FROM YELLOW RIBBONS TO A GOLD STAR

BIOGRAPHY OF A HERO: LCPL. DAVID R. BAKER, USMC

COMPILED BY: T-M FITZGERALD

D1522314

PublishAmerica
Baltimore

First printing

PublishAmerica has allowed this work to remain exactly as the author intended, verbatim, without editorial input.

Softcover 9781629078106
PUBLISHED BY PUBLISHAMERICA, LLLP
www.publishamerica.com
Baltimore

Printed in the United States of America

—PART I—

"Poor is the country that has no heroes, but beggard is the country that having them forgets."

—Unknown—

There've been books written, songs sung and legends born about men simply by virtue of their holding the title of veteran. There are notable names to list, names every American should be familiar with like Ronald Reagan, Audie Murphy and Clint Eastwood; veterans who became actors. And there would be other recognizable names; Chesty Puller, Omar Bradley, George Pershing, Gene Autry, Ira Hayes, Ernie Pyle, Maurice Brill—the list could continue for many pages. But it stops here. This is a book about another veteran; a young Marine named David Raymond Baker.

"All men are born equal. But then some become Marines." [9]

For less than ten percent of the population, there has been no worthier cause than to have raised their right hand and in their oath of enlistment, promise to defend the Constitution of the United States. From that percentage, fewer still have taken that oath with implicit intention of becoming a Marine:

"I, _____, do solemnly swear that I will support and defend the Constitution of the United States against all enemies foreign and domestic; that I will bear true faith and allegiance to the same; and that I will obey the orders of the President of the United States and the orders of the officers appointed over me, according to regulations and the Uniform Code of Military Justice. So help me God."

From the Halls of Montezuma,
To the shores of Tripoli;
We fight our country's battles
In the air, on land, and sea;
First to fight for right and freedom—
And to keep our honor clean:
We are proud to claim the title,
Of United States Marine.
Our flag's unfurled to every breeze,
From dawn to setting sun.
We have fought in every clime and place
Where we could take a gun;
In the snow and far-off Northern lands,
And in sunny tropic scenes;
You will find us always on the job—
The United States Marines.
Here's health to you and to our Corps,
Which we are proud to serve.
In many strife we've fought for life—
And never lost our nerve;
If the Army and the Navy—
Ever look on Heaven's scenes;
They will find the streets are guarded
By United States Marines.

———

—BECAUSE IT WAS TIME—

"I heard the voice of the Lord saying, 'Whom shall I send, and who shall go for us?' then said, "I, here am I: send me."

Isaiah 6:8

In 2007, author Robert Coram penned this in the biography he wrote; *American Patriot: The Life and Wars of Colonel Bud Day*:

"Military people are weepers. They weep when they watch a parade and the flag goes by. They weep when they hear the National Anthem. They weep at tales of valor and sacrifice. And as they get older, they weep at the memories of the brave men they have known." [9]

When determining how to assemble David Baker's biography, author (and family friend) T-M Fitzgerald had only a vague notion regarding how to begin. She swiftly began establishing a process for contacting various individuals from David's life and with permission from Baker's family, a page was set up on one of those well-known social networks gracing the Internet. Roughing out different outlines and ideas, it soon became clear that a more effective method would be required for Fitzgerald to weave the many accounts she was gathering into one, cohesive story about this Marine's life. Various questionnaires were developed and Fitzgerald stepped into hours of phone interviews. People spoke openly as she diligently wrote pages upon page of notes first in long-hand, then later transcribing their answers into mini manuscripts for them to review. Fitzgerald interviewed over sixty individuals across the span of five months but there still remained the question of how to weave everything she was told together. Who was she to change or delete any words David's acquaintances had elected to share? Instead of trying to manipulate various passages from those interview sessions into appropriately corresponding places throughout Baker's biography, Fitzgerald elected instead to transcribe the pages of hand-scribed notes she'd acquired, present each as a typed document to its' respective owner for review and then place each manuscript one-hundred percent as entrusted to her into the book.

Some interviews were from family members, some from friends and acquaintances but many from brothers David had served with in the United States Marine Corps and Navy. As varied as the individuals who granted the interviews, accounts ran the gamet from short and sweet to long and detailed. Many were wrought with raw emotion and included many off the record remarks and observations. Fitzgerald did not take a single word lightly as she listened to the stories shared by so many different walks of life. She was given to wonder how one man so young had touched so many in less than a lifetime.

Fitzgerald spoke with a wide range of individuals both military and civilian alike. No matter who she tried to contact, her efforts were limited to three attempts; with two exceptions. After the third unanswered request, Fitzgerald moved on because by then, she figured everybody knew how to contact her if they so desired.

For the vast majority of individuals Fitzgerald interviewed, the itemized list of questions she had devised proved almost unnecessary. The list proved to be merely a launching point, as once people began talking, the natural order of conversations went by what Fitzgerald had already intended to ask. During the interview processes, she was given privilege to hear many 'off the record' accounts in addition to the answers to base questions she had established. In the process, she gained a much deeper understanding of just what David R. Baker truly meant to his family, hometown friends and fellow Marines.

—FOR DAVID—

"And ye shall hear of wars and rumors of wars: see that ye be not troubled: for all these things must come to pass, but the end is not yet."

Matthew 24:6

As a writer crafts a story, he or she will occasionally stop and ask him or herself, "Do I really need all this background information? (Or back-story, such as it is called.)" Editors typically tell authors, *"Put it where it's needed."* Through the countless edits this biographical account went through, Fitzgerald deemed *all* the outwardly extemporary background information quite necessary for one reason; it was part of history; everybody's history. Remember; even though all his family, friends, fellow Marines and Navy Corpsmen knew the sources of each account shared here, this book was also meant to introduce David Baker to the *rest* of the world, to people who'd never been afforded opportunity to meet or know him, which invariably included people who never enlisted in the United States military.

If death is a possibility they undoubtedly are going to face, what is it then that still spurs hundreds of young men to join the military? Specifically, what drives so many to want to become Marines?

Although little over a generation separated the two sets of Marines and Corpsmen Fitzgerald was privileged to speak and consult with, certain characteristics among them remained unchanged. Take enlisting, for example. When asked why they decided to join the military, a random handful of Marines and Corpsmen answered that question as follows;

"I had two choices; go Air Force and be smart or go Marines and be tough. I had the opportunity to be better than what I was. I chose to be a Marine."

Another simply shared, *"My grandfather was a Marine in Korea. Hearing him tell all his stories sparked my interest."*

"I had friends who'd become Marines and decided to test myself, to see if I had what it took. I'm the first of my family who has been in the Marines and have no regrets."

"I joined because I was always fighting and that's what Marines do. I love my country and would do it all again. I'll tell anyone how the Corps taught me discipline and made a real man out of me."

"I knew when I was 16 that I wanted to be a Marine. It was something I had to do, I wanted to do. You know how you felt when you first fell in love and you knew that was the one? That's what I felt about the Marine Corps." (Incidentally, this particular Marine was still active duty at the time of his interview having served approximately 6 tours in combat.)

Perhaps the statement that summed it up best came from a Beirut era Marine: *"I'd decided if I was going to sign my life away, I wanted to do it wearing the Eagle, Globe, and Anchor, knowing that the Marines were and are the biggest, baddest mother-fuckers who ever walked this planet. I wanted to do something that had meaning, not fully understanding what or who I was about to become and what came with the title 'Marine'. It turned into becoming nothing about me and everything to do with living and fighting for my fellow Marines and this country"*

As far as everybody having tales of their own to tell, the world needs to consider that for every account told, different audiences are affected. How who reacts to what depends on the head atop that particular person's shoulders and what part of the story they heard.

Although given to grace others' lives for only a short period of time, Lance Corporal David Raymond Baker had without a doubt, time enough to leave behind a wealth of indelible impressions. His life would not be one defined by how he died but rather, how he lived. An 81mm mortarman (AKA 'An 81' so as not to be confused with being just *any* mortarman) for Weapons Company 1st Battalion, 5th Marines, (commonly referred to as the 'One-Five' (1/5) 1st Division, I Marine Expeditionary Force of Camp Pendleton, California), Baker was killed while supporting combat operations in the Nawa district of Afghanistan October 2009. (He wouldn't be given to witness the capture or subsequent death on 01 May 2011 of the man (Osama bin Laden) claiming to have masterminded the 2001 terrorist attacks on America.)

David had been looking forward to returning to his life and the world he thought he'd only temporarily left behind, anticipating going home to family and friends in Northeastern Ohio, settling back into civilian life and beginning pursuit of furthering his education. Instead, this Marine was killed a mere nineteen days following his twenty-second birthday. Baker died in a manner nobody anticipated, certainly in no way any young man enlisting in the Marines would have thought to imagine the first time he walked through a recruiter's door.

"I never know David," revealed Staff Sergeant Nickomar Santana, "—but his brother Mark, also a Marine, worked for me. "Mom (Laurie, Baker's mother) was distraught about everything." Santana paused, deep in thought. "It was absolutely crushing to hear what happened to David. I mean, it's awful *anytime* a Marine dies." The staff sergeant hesitated briefly "David was my brother, too. It was a real gut check to say the least."

By all accounts, LCpl. Baker wasn't a man destined to be remembered merely by his own family and friends. Instead, he was one of those individuals many have described as having that 'It' factor, a man one would expect whose biography would come at the end of a long, well-lived existence. Regarding David Baker, this biography is one that would undoubtedly have been written regardless had his life not been taken when it was. Instead, David became yet another Marine needing to be introduced to multitudes who'd never have the opportunity to meet him. As with all veterans whose lives have ended too soon, Baker's was a story *needing* to be told.

Aside from being a humble collection of memories and stories told by fellow Marines, Navy Corpsmen, family and friends, this Marine's biography was meant to share a life with a public who too soon forgets. Many wanted to ensure the life of one more Marine dyeing in service to this country would not go unnoticed or be overlooked. *"Numquam Obliviscar; Never Forget."* [14] This book was written because Baker himself wasn't granted the opportunity to collect his own memoirs and pen his own story as in the grand scheme of things should have been the case. It became an occasion denied to him by some unknown hand.

An understandably founded fear of this and assuredly any fallen Combat Veteran's parents is that their son would be forgotten. Gathering the numerous accounts creating the groundwork for this book, it was the authors' intent that *From Yellow Ribbons to a Gold Star* would lend definite surety that forgetting this Marine was never going to happen.

By perpetuating his life with an international standard book number and distinguishing his place among so many others in history, Fitzgerald wanted to do something more than vocalize overly used repartee in assuring Lance Corporal Bakers' family that their Marine's life would be remembered.

Fittingly enough, the United States Marine's gave the world this to consider; *"Semper Fidelis; Always Faithful."* For the totally chance circumstance a Marine named David R. Baker would became such a focus, Fitzgerald also wanted to give the world this to consider as well: *"Semper Conmemoro; Always Remember."* [Ibid.]

—YELLOW RIBBONS AND GOLD STARS—

"And what doth the Lord require of thee but to do justly, and to love mercy, and to walk humbly with thy God."

Micah 6:8

Countless narratives have been told which begin with references to yellow ribbons. (Too many of those accounts have ended with gold stars.) At a glance, such ribbons and stars are seemingly benign symbols with origins that many in society don't care to be acquainted with.

To begin with, yellow ribbons and gold stars are individually recognizable entities having strong affiliation with the military. Most people correctly associate these symbols with *remembering* something, but many aren't sure specifically what they're supposed to be remembering. One is displayed from perhaps personal obligation (possibly resulting from the latest community bandwagon effect) and the other is displayed to honorably acknowledge the most supreme sacrifice any member of the military and his/her family can make. Given the fact this is a book about a Marine, there's another iconic yellow symbol to consider that is perhaps equally if not more representative of David Baker; yellow footprints.

Some simply call them 'a Marine thing' and appropriately so. Before any young man's journey to turning into a Marine actually begins, there are yellow footprints to contend with. It doesn't matter which coast a recruit reports to for boot camp; Parris Island, South Carolina or MCRD in San Diego, California; if a man plans on becoming a Marine, he's got to get past the yellow footprints. It's standing within those prints, where thousands of others have stood before him, that a young man knows his life is about to change. *The Yellow Footprints* speech;

> *"You are now aboard Marine Corps Recruit Depot (MCRD) Parris Island South Carolina, and you have just taken the first step toward becoming a member of the world's finest fighting force, the United States Marine Corps."* [15]

Unfortunately, unless one is a veteran or has one in their life, familiarity with any of those symbols is appallingly dependent on how closely connected to an enlisted, deployed or deceased service member an individual may be. Take the yellow ribbons; for the most part, those decorative flashes of yellow and gold begin popping up on various landscapes for of one of two reasons; a where or a what; 'where' depending on the location a person happens to live and 'what' depending on what the majority of the neighbors are considering trendy at that particular point in time. These facts play major roles in when people might chance to see those patriotic displays. Understandably, outside of military communities, many people are not acquainted with the exact origin behind any of the customs and traditions colored in yellow. (Particularly the yellow ribbons; people see everybody else putting them out on display so they decide to start doing it, too.)

Depending where one may look for the information, it's not easy to pin down the exact source of those brilliant, flickers of yellow displayed in support of deployed military. Whether its actual yellow ribbons tied around anything and everything in sight or the substantial assortment of vehicle magnets that spontaneously appear on countless quarter panels and bumpers across the country, once those waves of yellow ignite, they spread like wildfire.

In the United States, some believe the practice of prominently placing yellow ribbons on display is remnant of a tradition originating as far back as the mid to late 1800's. Others believe the tradition began years after the Civil War following the release of a once popular song, 'Around Her Neck She Wore a Yellow Ribbon'. As soldiers from all branches of the military were sent on their various deployments, family members and friends left behind tied yellow ribbons on whatever was handy as visual reminders representing their hope and unspoken prayers for a loved one's safe return. [13]

A modern misconception is the yellow ribbon tradition stemmed not from any Civil War song but rather, after the 1973 Tony Orlando and Dawn hit, *Tie a Yellow Ribbon 'Round the Old Oak Tree.*

"The heroine in the song is waiting for her love to return home from prison. Her lover is about to be released and he writes a letter asking her to, 'tie a yellow ribbon 'round the old oak tree if you still want me.' He comes home and finds she has tied not one, but 100, yellow ribbons around the tree." [16]

Instead of being concerned with tracing exact origin of the tradition, perhaps an example would better define the convention.

A situation took place decades ago whereby a number of Americans were taken hostage in Iran. Back home in the United States, one hostage's spouse tied a large, yellow ribbon around a tree in front of their home in an observable display of hope regarding her husband's safe return. She told everybody the ribbon would stay on that tree until her husband untied it himself. Whatever the story about yellow ribbons may be, it didn't take long for the symbolic gesture to catch on with the rest of the country during the Iranian Hostage Crisis. [13]

So if only some can tell the actual lore behind all those yellow ribbons, fewer still can tell the story of the meaning behind the Gold Star. Walking any given street in America, a person may sooner or later chance to glimpse a modest sized red and white banner (called a service flag) on display in a window without understanding what it means. While some may allow their curiosity to peak and make an inquiry, others will simply favor remaining oblivious to what the meaning of any blue or gold star(s) sewn on that banner is meant to convey.

The Gold Star in and of itself has an impact all its' own. The 'American Gold Star Mothers, Inc.' site provided the following information;

> "During World War I, Blue Stars were used to represent each person, man or woman (who lived in that house) on active duty in Military Service to the United States. As war progressed and men were killed in combat, others wounded or died of their wounds or disease, there came about the accepted usage of the Gold Star. Whenever a

service member died, this Gold Star was substituted and superimposed upon those Blue Stars in such a manner as to entirely cover it. The idea of the Gold Star was that the honor and glory accorded the person for his supreme sacrifice in offering for his country, the last full measure of devotion and pride of the family in this sacrifice—" [3]

Gold Star. Though typically symbolizing the grieving mothers of fallen heroes, it isn't a club any mother (father, sibling, or other family member) elects to be an associate of. Though the star symbol has become synonymous with a grieving mother's heart, entire *families* have found themselves defined by the status. When a member of the United States military doesn't make it home, it's not only a mother's heart that grieves.

The Gold Star designation is not a title actively sought, but rather, one unexpectedly conferred. The least anybody 'from the outside looking in' can do is recognize what such a star hanging in those random windows means and recognize the fact somebody in that house died while serving in this country's military.

If a member of the military is killed in action (KIA) and his death isn't a matter of concern to civilians back home on a personal scale, then all too often the event claiming his life becomes a matter seemingly unworthy of concern or remembrance (except for one or two days of the year). *"Time marches on."* and *"Life continues."* Consensus seems to be if a person doesn't personally know the individual who died, why should it affect their life or matter anything to them? The point is, no matter who you are or who they are/were, the death of *any* member of our country's military should be a matter worthy of recollection to everyone; not only to that individual's family members and friends. If you don't believe this to be the case, think about the men who didn't make it home next time you go to the store or walk down the street and you aren't abducted and held for ransom. Think about them the next time you write a letter to the editor, or go to church and aren't persecuted for expressing an opinion or congregating with others in the name of organized religion.

FIRST, THERE WAS THE CIVILIAN.

(Then too briefly, the Marine.)

"Adversity teaches us things we cannot learn otherwise. It is your reaction to the adversity itself that determines how your (own) life's history will develop."

Dieter Uchtdorf

—THIS MARINE'S STORY—

"Two are better than one, because they have a good return for their work: if one falls down, his friend can help him up. But pity the man who falls and has no one to help him up."
Ecclesiastes 4:9-10

"I wasn't in his platoon but we did become close. He was a great guy; always had a smile on his face, always made people laugh. I'm sure EVERYONE remembers that smile. I go to his grave (at Arlington) whenever I get the chance."

(Armenta)

In early 2013, a number of schools across the nation debated teaching basic penmanship/cursive handwriting skills to students. (The rational assumedly being, *"What's the sense in actually writing a letter to anybody when you can send an e-mail instead?"*) In the throes of what the world wants to call progress, many great traditions have been lost or altogether abandoned. More often than not, people aren't interested in telling stories or writing letters. The days of story-telling at fireside gatherings or taking pride in writing beautifully scribed letters have gone by the wayside as implementation of new technology runs out of control. People can't/don't want to stop playing with their smartphones or gaming systems long enough to listen to a story much less be bothered with actually sitting down with pen and paper to write any kind of letter.

Autobiographies are the stories *everybody* knows, the tale every person can tell better than anyone else; their own life story. But what if a person can't tell their story? That story then becomes an account. *"It is what it is"* becomes *"It is what we tell you it was."* What you hold in your hands is a compilation of stories, memories, and events about a young Marine whose life ended too soon; taken. *From Yellow Ribbons to a Gold Star* is the account of a Marine who, as many have relayed, died, before his fullest potential was reached. It is a biography: the true account of a person's life written by somebody else except in this case, it's a compilation of stories told by many.

Frederick R. Barnard once said, *"A picture is worth a thousand words."* Words paint pictures, and a few well-thought out ones, such as the words in a book, the title itself or the headings of its' chapters can bring to mind a wealth of information about the subject long before a person has the opportunity to delve deep into the pages. Think of all the pictures and thoughts Barnards' seven words alone bring to life. A good title can tell a reader where a person has walked and what they have seen long before the pages are turned. *From Yellow Ribbons to a Gold Star* should evoke each of those points, particularly since those words are followed by *The Biography of a Hero: LCpl. David R. Baker, USMC.* This book is about an individual who possessed undeniable talent for boosting the determination, morale, and confidence of his fellow Marines; lifting ranks and drawing them together even during the worst of situations. This Marine embraced all of his brothers and could lift the heaviest of spirits when spirits were a heavy commodity to lift.

"Even the 'higher-ups' who'd come in for inspections, you know the kind of guys who aren't supposed to crack

a smile or chuckle out loud? David would do or say something at just the right moment and you'd see even those guys trying their damndest to keep from laughing. I never saw anybody else get away with doing that like Baker did."

1/5 Marine, 2012

So how does a person record the account of somebody's life he/she has never met? They do research, and lots of it. Inquiries and interviews become essential tools that cannot be ignored. Be it by family, friends, teachers, former bosses, or co-workers, no proverbial stone can be left unturned. Those stones aren't only proverbial, but essential.

People tend to take their everyday lives for granted, at least until something unpleasant happens; something so unimaginable, out-of-the-blue and unspeakable that makes our world stop turning. Such an event ultimately gives ground for a person to justifiably deliberate, "How can the rest of the world act so normal when I have to go through this?" Nobody thinks anybody outside their own microcosm cares enough to ask about their particular torment. Most people never start their day or begin a particular task thinking, "Maybe today, part of my life is going to be interesting enough for somebody to write about." But sometimes, when you least expect it, something happens to change all that.

Throughout time, hundreds of biographies have been written about members of the military; all-encompassing accounts about great men's lives detailing everything from their birth to whatever death they succumbed to. There are numerous biographies about individuals fortunate enough to have lived full, illustrious lives. Those are the books reading from top to bottom, inside and out. Those are the voluminous books that can be expected when a man reaches his 70's, 80's or beyond. By unfortunate contrast, no matter how deeply anybody reads into this Marine's biography, it only encompasses a comparatively short period of time, but a lifetime never the less. Because of that reason, if only one exceptional detail could be made perfectly clear, it would be this; in the space of barely twenty-two years, David Baker undeniably managed to accomplish what would by and large take a life-time for most other men to do. At the time of his death, David Baker wasn't a high-profile leader, he wasn't even an officer; but he could well have been both.

While reading about this Marine, it has to be understood what and who made David what he was and still is. Unlike many books about other Marines and military figures that have made it to the shelves of the local library, David's story is not one extolling any seemingly impossible military feat or marveling multiple tours of well-fought duty. Instead, his is a story derived from missions never taken, operations on which he would never deploy, opportunities that would never present themselves. This is a book about a Marine fated to never become part of any covert op or assigned any distinctive detail for the simple fact he wasn't given the luxury of time.

This biography is an attempt to show the rest of the world what they missed by never meeting this specific young man who so selflessly, willingly chose to represent this country; one of many who enlisted to fight a war that was a battle more for a concept than against any single person or country; freedom. Baker's biography should prove a reminder to what price we continue to pay for that seven-lettered word.

Paradox: *a statement leading to a contradiction which, if true, defies logic and reason.* [29] David Baker. His presence went beyond his physical years as many have attested, "*David had an old soul.*" Baker was a Marine who became a paradox, an enigma. "Matter can neither be created nor destroyed. It can only change form." Where did he come from? Is he still here? Is he really gone? It goes beyond the basic law of physics. The answer depends on who you ask. The United States Marine Corps? The Citizens of Painesville, Ohio? The Department of Defense? Census Bureau? Baker's family and friends?

> *"He was an angel from Heaven." His mother, Mama B. said with great emotion. "Angels love you and you just know it. David was like that. He gave hugs like an angel. He could walk into a room and instantly touch you. If ever a person could feel how it was to be embraced by an angel or God himself, that would be how I'd describe the way David touched people."*
>
> Mama B.

As any Marine and other members of the military can attest to, *"Always have a backup plan because the first one probably won't work."* [7] David had insight, and perhaps more than anybody realized, knew the need for such preparation. But who could know how truly prepared he was to be? Baker was a God-fearing man who firmly believed in his faith, his country and Corps. Baker was a Marine who knew he wasn't coming home.

First and foremost, he knew he had a job to do. No matter how bad the state of affairs or current situation would turn or how sorry anybody was feeling during any particular mission or assignment, LCpl. Baker was generally the guy who'd turn things around. Never losing sight of the task at hand, David would pull the worst out of any situation and make it more bearable, all the while doing his part to make sure everybody made it back alive. As more than one of his fellow Marines stated, *"He could turn a bad situation around without even realizing it. That was who he was and that was enough."*

"On one hand, you know it's a possibility (death), but you don't want to admit to it; like, just admitting it could happen will cause it to happen. But on the other hand, if you don't acknowledge it, it's like it can't happen. I don't know how else to say it. David knew. He knew. He somehow seemed already at peace with maybe not coming home."

Mark Baker, brother, 2012

—IMPRESSIONS—

"In my Father's house are many mansions: if it were not so, I would have told you. I go to prepare a place for you."

John 14:2

"Time: a commodity none of us are sure of; because tomorrow is guaranteed to no one." [9] Too often, it turns out the events a Combat Marine wants to remember least are the moments he cannot forget. Because of this outwardly contradictory fact, the world itself needs reminding of the many losses connected to war, losses which can never be recovered; physical and mental pain that will never ease, life-affecting injuries, some which may never be visible. Most importantly, there should be reminders, tribute paid to those who lost their lives.

In a history defined by prominent battles, illustrious campaigns, amphibious landings and all-out war,[32] the casualties of war are everybody's casualties to bear. *"Out of sight, out of mind"* seems the mantra many choose to subscribe to. Problems only exist if people confront them. *"This isn't my problem and I don't have to confront it. Life goes on"* and sure, all of this is correct; but only to a certain extent.

Take the multiple terroristic acts of 9-11 and consider the World Trade Center alone. How many thousands of people died there? In the days following the attacks, American flags could be seen flying everywhere. Patriotism and pride were at incredible levels. Though how long did it take for the massive tide of flags and pride to recede and seemingly evaporate? How long did it take for America's patriotism to taper off, dissipate and gradually disappear? Who remembers September 11th, 2001 wasn't even the *first* time the World Trade Center had been attacked? Who can recall the number of casualties stemming from the first attack or the date it happened? The name of a single victim from either event? Chances are, unless you were personally affected, that information isn't part of your general knowledge base.

"(Marines) sign up knowing the risk. Those innocent people in New York didn't go to work thinking there was any kind of risk." [1]

"*Everybody* has a story." Remember those four words. One must remember even significant expectations aren't always met and things we think should exist often don't. In the very least, a good story will generate curiosity, particularly when it's about an extraordinary person or event. But curiosity doesn't last. Just like all the patriotism post 9-11, curiosity eventually tapers off, evaporates, and disappears. A few books make it past the E-reader stage and onto actual shelves. Some of those have even become best-sellers. But sadly, it appears only books about 'high profile' individuals or events are what get the shelf space. What happens to the stories about the other guys? Other heroes who came, who saw, and excelled at what they did? What about all those men who went, who saw, but didn't return? Why are more people not speaking for them? People forgot and over time, too many stories of great men have never seen the light of day.

If an account such as Baker's biography were created for each life taken in defense of this country, people could expect libraries across the nation to house entire sections, or at least have dedicated multiple shelves to all the heroes this nation has lost; but they don't. Therein lays the obligation, and responsibility. It's up to people those heroes leave behind to remember and appreciate their sacrifice, to never forget who fought and died serving this land. Sadly, despite the fact there are so many, countless names have become mere statistics with the passing of each day. There should be a desire to learn more about these men, men whose deaths were once broadcast in reverent tones on the nightly news, men whose names used to be announced so routinely but eventually started being read from day-old postings (if they were read at all). It wasn't because anybody declared an official end to the events taking place overseas, but more that announcing names of any fallen had become a matter less of importance to those who preferred to remain uninvolved. Despite the fact that men continued to die, nobody was hearing the names anymore.

—'B'; HIS NAME IS BAKER'—

"He carried his own baby picture around and would tell everybody, 'I'm the cutest baby there is.'"

Mama B.

Before a child is born, parents visualize a clearly defined future; certain things that are supposed to happen at certain times along the way. First, there may be a few baby showers for Mom before the big event, the birth and naming of the child then bringing little one home to show to family and friends. After all the hoopla of baby's arrival subsides, there's that collective list of firsts everybody anticipates; the first time baby turns over, first words spoken, first teeth, and those momentous first steps. There's first day of school, maybe a first field trip, some braces, then first car, prom and before they all know it, time for graduation. That little baby has grown up and it's time to make a decision about college or which branch of the military and maybe marriage to look into; but it doesn't end there.

Parents look forward to imparting pearls of wisdom on to each child they bring into the world, assuming each of their children's lives will follow the preconceived order we all expect. As one generation passes, the next will step into place. While all that seems good and well, it's not necessarily what the child envisions for him/herself, at least not right away. While Mom and Dad relish those idyllic images of their baby's future, every so often, the ambitions they set for their child get reprioritized, especially when wee-one is a son who grows up, recognizes his own aspirations and makes a trip to the local Marine recruiter's office.

Long before war in '*The Stan*' (Afghanistan) began, Americans already knew about Arlington, Virginia and its' white, marble headstones in perfectly aligned rows. The whole world knew about American Marines, too. "Semper Fi!" and "Ooh-rah!" But outside of families and friends, how many knew any of the faces of freedom? Names of men who died for this country during '*Operation Enduring Freedom*' (OEF) alone in Iran, Iraq, and Afghanistan? How many knew anything about the sacrifices of families they left behind? In America, people reluctantly came to be acquainted with the flag-draped transfer cases and caskets ceremoniously carried from planes in Dover, Delaware The public seemed slow to realize, (through not due entirely to fault of their own) that there was a war going on and a lot of young men weren't coming home. [8]

The Fallen; from the outside looking in, many people *think* they knew them. They were the young men who went from graduating high school to "*making it through the rigors of boot camp and deployment.*" They were the same ones people began reading about in local papers who became "*Marine Lain to Rest*" or the "*Marine Awarded Purple Heart Posthumously.*" The Fallen were men from seemingly obscure places like Moose Pass, Alaska and Presque Isle, Maine. They hailed from Yuma, Arizona and Billings, Montana, as well as Chicago and Byron, Illinois. They came from territories, Commonwealths and every state in the nation, including Ohio, specifically, a town located outside Cleveland on the shores of Lake Erie called Painesville.

As of 31 May 2013, the number of American casualties stemming from Operation Enduring Freedom was reported to be in the thousands with most of those losing their lives ranging between the ages of 18 and 24.[7] Shamefully enough, the deaths of many of these service-members became little more than faceless data to anyone outside their families. Thanks to the Bush Administration, the media was initially limited to what it was they were allowed to report; Americans were effectively desensitized to the war, over-saturated instead with those mundane filler stories the news agencies were allowed to report regarding the war abroad. Soldiers and Marines simply became 'the fallen;' and those killed in the line of duty were flown to Dover under the cover of darkness so nobody could witness their return. [8] Each return should have been a homecoming. Indisputably heartbreaking, each death should have been more than a statistic to forget or some inconvenient reminder of war merely brushed from thought. Unfortunately their deaths became more a matter of 'out of sight, out of mind.'

Unfortunately, because of the ban on media coverage enacted by the Bush Administration in 1991 during the first Gulf War, [30] news reports broadcasted into America's living rooms each night were essentially censored stories, telling Americans exactly what the government wanted them to hear. For all intent and purposes, citizens of the United States were numbed to actual events that took place in Afghanistan, Iran and Iraq. In the years following the initial outbreak of war, it was argued that the reason such a ban had been put into place was specifically to keep Americans from knowing the true cost of war. Instead of using the media to educate people, it was used to manipulate them instead. It wasn't until March of 2003 that the current presidential administration finally lifted the eighteen year ban that had prevented media from covering the return of America's soldiers and Marines. That's when the war 'over there' finally became real over here; at least for a little while.

The return of flag-draped caskets should have prompted the good people back home in America who were busy enjoying their freedoms into recognizing those freedoms came at profound cost. The losses of those men should have served as reminders that this country remains free only because of individuals willing to protect and defend from their own accord what this nation has stood for, voluntarily willing to protect it in the name of millions they will never know or meet. Like thousands of Marines before him, David Baker stepped up, signed the line, and joined a military less than nine percent of the country's population becomes part of. [Ibid.] Baker did not opt to join just any branch. He chose to become one of the few, the proud; a United States Marine and ultimately died for his convictions. While being a mortar man (an '81) for the 1/5 ("One-Five") wasn't his first choice of jobs, David was determined to serve his country despite the fact that war was actively taking place at the time he enlisted. It's generally a given that any man who enlists in a combat MOS (military occupational specialty/job) during active war is guaranteed to see battle in a way he may have never imagined.

Marine. What image does that word invoke? When asked about United States Marines, society in part may think of stoic, chivalrous individuals. Many picture the distinguished uniforms, those sharply pressed dress blues and the men wearing them with nary a thread nor hair out of place. While he is all those things, a Marine is a defender first and foremost. ("The Marine Corps is the only branch of the U.S. Armed Forces that recruits people specifically to fight.") [18]

Marines are a possessed lot. (After all, did the Germans not designate them 'teufel hunden' (devil dogs) when they took Belleau Wood?) They may be possessed but they're an incomparable lot and as such, each worthy of tales of their own. By the very virtue of being a Marine, they are (and remain) united across generations. "Leave no man behind." Not even death separates members of this family. It's more than the common journey stemming from those yellow footprints that bonds Marines.

Men (and women) who've earned the title United States Marine extol and inspire certain ideals and values such as pride and camaraderie, so much to the extent that accounts spring up from Hollywood regularly. We've all watched the movies and have seen the end results. We've read the life accounts about exemplary Marines who went to war, became survivors of POW camps or mass fire fights in various campaigns, recipients of bronze stars or the Medal of Honor. But what about the men who didn't? What about the others? Those whose lives were taken, *stolen* while they were performing their everyday jobs? It doesn't appear Hollywood has thought to make a movie about any of those men yet.

Who remembers the names of those who've died doing the ordinary? The ones who died without warning but for the same exact purpose; doing a job they were sent to do. In any circumstance regarding a United States Marine, you can guarantee their Marine brothers will remember; their families and friends will remember. In the very least, the death of Lance Corporal Baker proved to those he left in this world that for a time, their world was a brighter place for having him in it.

They went with songs to battle, they were young
Straight of limb, true of eyes, steady and aglow—
They were staunch to the end against odds uncounted,
They fell with their faces to the foe.

They shall not grow old as we that are left grow old.
Age shall not weary them, nor will the years condemn.
At the going down of the sun and in the morning,
We will remember them.[6]

—AMAZING—

"Blessed are the peacemakers: for they shall be called the children of God."

Matthew 5:9

David Raymond Baker was the second son born to Laurie and Mark Baker. (However, David was not the only child in the family to choose the military path. He wasn't even his family's' only Marine.) Before yellow footprints or yellow ribbons became commonplace for those who knew him, there was Baby Boy Baker. Due to unanticipated medical circumstances, little 5lb 12oz David Raymond Baker came into this world nearly four weeks before he was due.

"I had a condition called placenta previa and instead of the end of October or the beginning of November, we got our little bundle of joy on October 1st. After David was born, I only got to see him for maybe a second before they whisked him away. They ended up giving me a room at the end of the hall, farthest from the nursery. I later found out they weren't sure he was going to make it through the night.

I was always afraid someone was going to come to the hospital and kidnap my babies, and with David being so far down the hall from me, I was worried about that. When I walked down to look into the nursery window at my child, the only thing I saw was that he wasn't there. I immediately started crying. A nurse came out and asked what was wrong and of course, I told her I'd thought somebody had taken my baby. She asked my baby's name and assured me nobody had taken him. They were getting him ready to bring him to me. Since I was already at the nursery, I asked if I could walk him back.

As I pushed his little bed back to my room, other mothers who'd heard me crying earlier were standing in their doorways, clapping as we walked by. And you know, now that I'm thinking about this, people did that for him at the airport, too when he come home on leave. When I would take him back to the airport, people stood and clapped then, as well. (They did for Mark and Lauren, too.) But at the hospital, those moms were standing there, clapping for him, commenting how he was such a pretty baby. They were all so happy for us. Come to find out, apparently they'd heard there was a baby who might not make it through the night and had figured out it was my David."

"*Real heroes don't wear capes or numbers. They wear dog tags.*" [32] Baker's was not a life long-lived, but he left it a hero. He did not die in some characteristically Hollywood fashion whereby the bad guys were caught and the good guys rode off into the sunset. He wasn't involved with any clandestine missions in obscure locals. His death was a matter of location and timing. It mattered more what he died for than how he died. "*Freedom isn't free.*" For that, Baker paid the ultimate price.

All veterans are heroes; most being of the reluctant variety, Marines in particular. They are quick to correct you, fiercely loyal to their Corps. But when it comes to acknowledging their part in keeping this country free, even the craggiest of them all may blush and quietly state "*I was just doing my job.*"

"He's a hero. He didn't have to die in Afghanistan to be my hero, though."

Mark Baker, Sr./David's father-2009 [21]

Baker was an ideal Marine; Leatherneck, Devil Dog. Although he'd never achieve the titles of husband or father, or have the luxury of completing any college degree, Baker was still a son, a grandson, brother, and friend. Before the man or the Marine, there were other things that David was (and still is), more attributes than adjectives; humorous, warm, out-going, jovial, gregarious, fun-loving, crazy, courageous, confident, serious, and genuinely caring. Just weeks away from completing his combat tour, David's life was taken while he was doing the ordinary. Only for Marines in Afghanistan, (or wherever location their duty station may see them) doing the 'ordinary' was anything but.

Joyful, dauntless, courageous and exemplary; adjectives and attributes used to describe LCpl. David Baker. In determining to create this book, a mass family meeting was required. In October of 2012, that meeting came into fruition as the author made a visit to northeastern Ohio procuring the opportunity to begin speaking with members of David's immediate family.

A few were gathered at the dining room table, and a couple stood in the kitchen. One maintained post in the living room. With a nephew and niece that Baker never had opportunity to meet keeping the session lively, members of David's family formed a happily chaotic and amazingly dynamic lot. (Author's note: *"I was certainly made to feel welcomed by this energetic and lively family. Their reception gave me a deeper appreciation of one aspect regarding the kind of background David came from."*) What follows is the flow of conversation from that roundtable discussion, questions asked and answered about the son, the brother, and fellow Marine.

How would you describe the city you've all grown up in, Painesville Ohio to people interested in learning about where David came from?

Taylor: "Describe Painesville? It depends. We're not a huge place but we're not very small, either. We're not far from Cleveland and we're not what you'd call out in the country. I'd say we were somewhere right in the middle. It's an area of working class people who happen to live by a really big lake."

Lauren: "You'll meet some interesting people here, too. David was definitely one of them." David's sister spoke with great fondness as her twin nodded mutually in silent agreement.

Where did David do most of his growing up?

Mama B.: "With his dad. But on weekends he'd be over to the house, at least until him and Markie got their licenses. Then they were at our house every day and staying overnight." Mama B. looked at her daughters. "Everyone knew the girls as 'Baker's Sisters.'"

Mark: "Hmmm, growing up with David." He laughed. "He played baseball for forever. We'd play outside; you know, ride our bikes and stuff like that because it was just me and him. We didn't have friends around the house to play with because we went to private school and all the kids who went to Zion either rode bus or were driven to school by their parents. So I mean, we had friends at school, but at home, we just had each other."

When asked what kind of music David favored, everybody spoke at once:

"Oh God. He liked everything. He listened to Gangsta Thugs, Bone Thugs and Harmony of Cleveland, Tupac, and Dr. Dre. He listened to Billy Joe Shaver, too (*Live Forever*) and liked Tim McGraw and his song '*Next Thirty Years*'."

"And '*Don't Take the Girl*,'" Mama B. interjected thoughtfully from her post in the living room. "—he really liked that song."

Mark: "He listened to Rehab, too." David's older brother added from his place at the dining room table. "And Kings of Leon for a while. He liked everything."

Lauren: "I'm sure none of his friends knew this," David's sister started to snicker, "—but David also liked listening to Britney Spears. He had Taylor make him a poster of her one time. He'd sing her songs out loud. I mean, we'd sing Britney songs to our brother while we were all sitting in the big beanbag chair with headphones on. That was fun."

Mama B.: "That reminds me. I haven't explained the story behind the song '*Chicken Fried*' yet." Baker's mom smiled as she readied to share the tale. "I don't much care for talking too much on the phone. So I asked all the kids what their favorite song was so I could make that song their ringtone. That way, whenever they called, I'd always know who it was and would be sure to answer the phone. We weren't allowed to use personal phones at work but whenever I heard one of my kids' songs, I didn't care, I'd answer. One day, David happens to call from California and I asked him what his favorite song was. Well, he was quiet for a minute before he answered. '*Have you ever heard the song 'Chicken Fried' by the Zac*

Brown Band?' That's my favorite song. My favorite part is where they sing about saluting the ones who died'" I told him, 'That's going to be your ring tone.' Every time he called, that's how I knew it was him."

Eyes brimming with tears, Mama B. continued. "From that point on, every number David called me from, I'd program that song as his ring tone." Mama B. paused. "Sometimes I still text his old number. Whether it goes through or anybody gets it, I don't know but I still text him." Mama B. wiped her eyes. "Anyway, that's part of why they played that particular song the entire day of his memorial service. That and the fact a certain controversial church had plans to come here and protest his funeral," A detectable flash of anger flickered in her eyes. "—and they *were* here, you know. But everybody kept them away. We never had to see any of them."

I've asked Marines who served with David to list some adjectives they'd use to describe him. What might be some you would use?

Lauren: "Adjectives describing my brother—" Giving a giggle that turned into a broad smile, Baker's sister asked, "Can I use a little profane language here? As far as adjectives go, how about asshole? And I mean that in every sense of the word possible, too." Lauren paused thoughtfully. "Now you know I am his sister, after all so I say that as only a sister could." She sat back, a smile still playing at the corners of her mouth. "Let me give you an example. One time at school, he decided to take my books, *willingly* take my books and walk me to class. So we get there and he had the nerve to ask me for money for doing it. I was like, 'Money? I don't have any money.' So he took my Juicy Fruit gum instead."

Taylor: "My turn." David's other sister chimed in. "I want to say 'good'; David was a good big brother. He was always nice to me."

Lauren interjected: "And why do you think he was always so nice to you? Because you'd tell him fibs about me! I'm so oblivious to things going on around me. One time, you told him I didn't say hello to you or something and what did he decide to do? Throw my shoes up over a wire," Laurens face broke into a grin. "—apparently just because I didn't say hi."

Taylor: "Once when I was upset and crying at school," Taylor paused. "—I mean, because of other things going on at the time, David happened to be walking by. He saw me and was like, *'What's going on? What's wrong?'* He looked at whatever teacher it was going by, held his hand up and said, *'I got this, I got this.'*"

Lauren: "Sure. He was all protective of *you* maybe but it was more, *'Fend for yourself, Lauren'* to me." She paused in thought. "Well, no, not always. There was one time he called me a G.I. Joke." she spoke making reference to her enlistment in the Army. "He was probably jealous." She smiled affectionately, her eyes sparkling. "Here's another adjective; humorous. David was definitely humorous."

Mama B. quickly agreed, "Humorous. Definitely, yes. He had a sarcastic, but honest sense of humor."

Conversation turned next to significant turning points in David's life...

Mama B.: "As for turning points—" Mama B. paused in reflection. "I'd have to say graduating from 'Our Shepherd Parochial School' and 9-11. That made a huge impact on him."

Taylor: "When he told us he was joining the Marine Corps, I was like, 'Ha! So you're gonna be a Marine.' It never occurred to me something bad could happen to him. I mean, I knew what was going on over there but was more concerned with high school and boys, you know? Teenage stuff."

Mama B.: "Remember I told you about JonBenet Ramsey and how he was so heartbroken over what happened to her? David was beside himself. *'How could anyone kill somebody like that? Harm a little girl?'* He kept up with her story all over the news. It was awful for him, like he knew her, or it was his own sister or something. It affected him that much."

Taylor: "David was the type of person who'd feel your pain with you."

Mama B.: "He was the guy who'd always have your back."

Lauren: "I had to have been about 15 or 16 years old. One of my friends had come over to spend the night and we'd decided to sneak outside for a smoke. We went out and lit up; leaving the door opened a crack so we could get back in after we finished. Well, Mom put the dogs out and of course, when she let them back in she walked by the front door and shut it; all the way. Then locked it. Thank God I had my cell phone with me." Lauren glanced at her mother and started laughing. "I wasn't about to knock on the door because I wasn't ready to die" she joked (in reference to getting caught smoking). "So I called David. Remember, this was almost midnight. I finally got hold of him and he tells me, *'You're going to have to wait until I get home. I'll be there in an hour.'* That wouldn't have been so bad except I had to go to the bathroom; really bad—" She trailed off as her face broke into another broad grin. "That reminds me," She brought up another occasion. "—of the first time David caught me smoking. He didn't tell. Instead, he taught me how to smoke like a man. That was so cool of him. He was so funny." She paused as she remembered.

Mama B.: "Let me tell about the first time I caught David smoking. It was the girls' 13th birthday. I remember this so well because Taylor was MIA (missing in action) from some Halloween thing. We were out everyplace looking because I thought somebody took her."

Lauren: "You heard that, right? They were out looking for Taylor—"

Taylor: "I was actually safe and sound." She interjected happily.

Mama B.: "It was October 15, sometime after midnight. David and I were driving all over the place looking for Taylor. He was up at the Fairgrounds and I was getting ready to have an Amber Alert put out. So I go up there, pull into the Fairgrounds and there sits David, lighting up a cigarette. I looked at him and asked, 'You smoke?' And he shoots back, '*Ma, my sister is missing. What do you expect?*' He was in a panic looking for her."

Lauren: "Hah! See? He panicked for YOU!"

Taylor: "Well, I was the baby."

Mama B.: "You remember that time those boys put you in the trunk of the car and David went out looking for them? They were more afraid of him then of the Lake County Sherriff."

Lauren: "David told us stopping at stop signs outlined in white was optional." She grinned. "And you know, right, all stop signs are outlined in white?" David's sister smiled as she continued. "He threatened to throw me out of the car once. We were somewhere in Painesville on the way to a friends' house. He actually took the seat belt off me and I thought for sure he was going to do it." Pausing as she reminisced, Lauren continued her story. "David was taking me to another friend's house this other time but decided he needed to go get cigarettes first. On the way, he sees his friend Josh and the two of them decide to race to the stoplight. Scariest thing in my life. We get there, he gets his smokes and they decide to race all the way back. That's not where it stopped, though. No, he decided to pull the e-brake and we ended up doing a complete 180. No lie! I about shit my pants."

"David was the one who told me not to go active duty, so because of him, I didn't. But he sure made fun of me a lot. You know, brother sister stuff. Like, take this for example. I have hazel eyes, right? Well, David's were blue. On the way home from the MEPS after Mark joined the Marines, David and I had this stupid argument about blue eyes and hazel eyes. He argued his point just for the sake of arguing. Like, *'Lauren? What color is the sky? It's blue. See? My eyes are blue, the sky is blue.'* It was this ongoing battle about nothing, just for because."

"David wanted to go out one time. Mark was getting ready to go somewhere and was taking his good old, sweet time in the shower. It wasn't too long before David got tired of waiting and came up with this plan. He was like, *'Lauren, come up to the bathroom with me.'* So of course, I went. Then what did he do but literally pull Mark out of the shower and throw him into the linen closet. He told me, *'Sit down right here and don't look.'* There I was with both my brothers, sitting in front of the door so Mark couldn't get out." Lauren paused before she giggled. "After he got done in the shower, David yelled out, *'On the count of three, RUN!' 1-2-RUN!'* So he jumped out of the shower and started running. Talk about awkward." She nodded to herself. "And have I told you about the time he made me eat grass?"

Mama B.: "David was very protective but you know, his friends and family were, are still just as protective of him." As she said this, the girls emphatically shook their heads in agreement. Mama B. added, "The girls were protective of David."

Taylor: "Talking about painting pictures of David with words, well I told you he was a good brother," Taylor took a deep breath, exhaling slowly as she continued. "—but he was so much more. We were at school this one time, and he didn't want to go to class, so he decided to walk me to mine." Taylor paused before she spoke again. "And he'd always drive me to school. I didn't go to first-period half the time because I had math and I hated math. So one winter day, David was like, '*Hey, you want to go to class?*' Of course, I said no, so we ended up staying home the first hour of school that day watching '*How the Grinch Stole Christmas.*'

Lauren: "There was another time we were on the way to school and we ended up spinning out on the ice." Lauren paused as she remembered. "David and I went to a friend's going-away party together, this graduation thing in Painesville. He told me, '*Don't tell anybody I'm your brother. Just say I'm some friend of yours.*' Well, there was this guy there who liked me and he started asking about David, 'Are you two together?' I told him no and," She trailed off, eyes beginning to brim with tears. "Just stuff like that all the time." Despite the humor she started sharing her memories with, it was obvious they were hard to talk about. "David would be like, '*Hey, let's go to Steak-and-Shake.*' So there we'd go. I remember one time when we were driving down the street and all of the sudden, he decided to cover my eyes! I mean, while I was driving, no less. So I hollered at him, 'What are you doing?' He didn't think anything of it and real calmly asked, '*What? Can't you* *multi-task?*' We eventually made it to the Stake-and-Shake, alive. We went in and spent time chillin'. There were lots of times like that; times we didn't do anything specific but where we still had a lot of fun."

"One time, it was about 100F degrees outside and we were driving somewhere when David decided to turn the heat up and lock all the doors. Then he started going about ten miles an hour. Markie held the back door open which didn't help that much but," Lauren paused sheepishly. "I guess it was something I think was funny. The four of us always had lots of typical brother and sister stuff going on. And like Mom said, David was protective, sometimes too much. One time, he told me and Taylor that he didn't want us hanging out with any of his friends but I guess he thought about it a bit because he changed his mind and decided it was okay. I think it was because he knew them and thought it was probably the safer thing. David acted like any big brother would. As we got older, we formed alliances. He'd watch UFC (Ultimate Fighting Championship) and practice on Taylor and I—"

Taylor: "We got pretty good at blocking and defending and all that kind of stuff." Taylor interjected quietly. "But now, it's just Me, Lauren, and Mark." Taylor stood beside her chair. "I think it was the following Christmas when I wanted to do another family picture for Mom, but of course, David was already gone. Our aunt had shirts made with David's picture on them and the three of us had a portrait done for Mom for her birthday."

Mama B.: Do you remember the time we played Trivial Pursuit? David got the question where he had to name the only country that began with the letter 'A' but didn't end in 'A'. None of us could think of the answer. We finally looked it up,

and of all places, it was Afghanistan. He was like, '*Where the hell is that*?' The irony of it all, David died in Afghanistan."
A subdued hush fell across the room as everyone pondered the thoughts on the tips of their tongues. Baker's brother broke the silence.

Mark: "Remember that time at the church? David and I were sitting in the back tying the strings on that one guy's hoodie together—" Laughing heartily in recollection, he exclaimed "Man, we were hammered, too. The pastor had asked for everybody to rise. David jumped up and shouted, '*FIRST*!'"

Lauren: "After he died, we were all sitting together for his service in Arlington. When they asked for everyone to rise, we decided it'd be funny to shout out '*FIRST*!' So we did and we weren't quiet about it, either." The girls giggled as they recounted the story. "People gave us the dirtiest looks. Markie and Mike Hatton were trying so hard not to laugh. It was funny." Lauren's voice turned softer. "You know, when we were all at Arlington, I saluted him. I mean, I didn't talk to anybody. I didn't want to be a part of it. To think about what happened to David, I still get mad, so angry. I felt so much disbelief and anger and well, it's hard to describe."

Taylor: "I was in my first semester at college when David was killed. I'm surprised I even passed because I missed two weeks of class. I remember sitting there thinking about everything. David was never going to hold my baby. He'd never get to be the wonderful uncle I knew he was going to be. All that bothered me—" Taylor paused "—it still does."

Mama B. took that moment of pause as opportunity to speak. "That reminds me of something else. One time when David was home on leave, he did this," She stood up and made motions in the air as if to measure somebody tall, medium, small, and someone holding a baby. "I asked him what that was and he said, '*That's me and my family. It's me, my wife, my son, and my daughter.*' Then he says, '*Mom, what's this?*' and she lay down on the floor with her arms across her chest to demonstrate what David had done. "I told him I didn't know and asked him what it was? He said, '*It's me in my casket.*'" She said softly.

Lauren: "I remember that, I *remember* him doing that. He knew. I mean, he knew."

Mama B.: "He did all that before he was deployed to Afghanistan."

Do you know if David had any near brushes with death or witnessed—

Taylor quickly interrupted: "We never really asked him about that."

Mama B.: "Well, there were a few stories David told me. One was how they'd been driving in their Hummer on patrol and they'd stopped somewhere. From what I understand is for some reason or other, they got an uneasy feeling so they backed the truck up. A little later, an RPG (rocket propelled grenade) went off right where the truck had been parked. Then there was another time when they had to go get somebody and they hit an IED (improvised explosive device) with the back of the truck. Nobody was hurt but that was the second time. If I remember this correctly, there were also a couple of times some Afghani National almost shot him. David jumped at the right moment and…" Mama B. paused in quiet reflection.

David Baker was a man whose life, though short lived, was defined by the most comprehensive adjective of all; United States Marine.

—BEFORE HE WAS A MARINE—

"Courage is endurance for one moment more."
Unknown 2nd Lt. Marine, Vietnam

When Baby David came home from the hospital, big brother Markie was ready. Baker's brother was going through serious health issues of his own when David was born. So even though Markie was, as Mama B. put it, "—pretty sick, he was excited about being a big brother. Markie always wanted to help me with David, and he did. He was a good big brother. He loved Baby David."

From the moment they became brothers, the Baker Boys were what their father called "polar opposites" when it came to their individual personalities and characteristics. Mark was always the more rambunctious one while David was labeled more reserved.

"I would say Mark was high-strung where David was more low-key." Spending their formative years with their father, Mr. Baker had more than a few stories to share about how the boys occupied their time.

"Mark absolutely loved his little brother. He and David looked so much alike that people often mistook them for twins, and boy how they hated that. (Not quite two years separated the Baker brothers.) By the time David was born, Mark was already hitting his developmental milestones; those monumental firsts, doing everything earlier than most kids his age. He walked before he was eight months old and started riding bike early as well. He was a very busy little boy. Then along came David who was all quiet and shy. He was content with watching big brother Mark do his thing. And as I've said, Mark was the more outgoing one, so much in fact that for the longest time, he would actually speak for David. David would sit quietly, and let Mark tell us if he needed or wanted anything. We started getting worried something might be wrong with David because for the longest time, he didn't talk." Mark Baker, Sr. commented when asked about the boys growing years. "But I guess he grew out of that."

When questioned about the kind of life he hoped his boys would lead, Mark did not hesitate to answer.

"For the most part, their lives went the way I wanted for both of them. But with David, well his was going the way I had envisioned but," Mr. Baker stopped abruptly "I don't make the rules in the world."

"I suppose they'd both say I was a strict father, that I made them practice responsibility. I saw them both finishing school, going to college, being successful in doing whatever it was they decided to do."

"It was important to me that they both received a Christian education, so they attended parochial school at the Zion Lutheran church. I remember David coming home one day, I think it was around fourth grade, with this paper asking, 'What do you want to be?' He'd written, 'Marine.' I guess I tried dissuading him even back then, but you see what happened? They both joined the Marines anyway."

How did you feel when David told you he enlisted?

"Both of them enlisted but it was David who actually persuaded Mark to sign up." Mr. Baker paused "David enlisted first. Mark had been doing his clinical work at the time and decided to quit and join the Marines. It was David's senior year when we had a talk about all of that. I think they both kept it from me as long as they possibly could before sitting down to tell me. Mark might say differently, but that's kind of how I felt. A parent always wants the best for their kids. I mean, that's the point, right?" Mr. Baker's voice turned melancholy.

When asked about the boys' upbringing, Big Mark revealed in an easy, laid-back manner that he, himself was a native of Saginaw, Michigan. He shared how as a child, he had spent a lot of time at a family cottage on the lake. Having grown up in that area, Big Mark wanted to instill the same memories and traditions to his boys.

"I was born and raised in Saginaw. I still have many childhood friends; great memories of Michigan; lots of family ties. I wanted the boys to have that too. Living in Ohio, we'd always go up there to the lake for the summer. Even as grown men, they had friends they'd grown up with who still lived there. It was fun for them." Taking a brief pause to collect his thoughts, Big Mark continued. "I tried keeping them involved in sports as much as possible, as well. I guess I tried imparting how my life had gone onto the boys. They played a lot of ball, attended parochial school," Mark stopped again. "That was a bigger transition for me then the boys, sending them to public high school after parochial. The kids from Zion completed their transition together. Everybody knew each other so it was no problem for them."

At first, it didn't sound easy for Baker's father to respond to the questions presented to him about his youngest son. It was evident how much thought Big Mark was putting into each answer. As the conversation continued, Mark, Sr. began speaking more candidly.

"When David was little, he had all these action figures; I mean a ton of them. He'd come home from school every day and go off and play Army or whatever with those figures for hours at a time, I mean every day. In school, on and off they'd have the Youth thing going on; of course, this was on top of all the other things little boys do when they're growing up."

"The day we moved into our house, this one kid came over. I mean, we were in the middle of bringing our belongings in and here comes this kid on his bike. I guess he decided he needed to see what was going on over here so he came skidding into the driveway sideways and walks straight into the house. I thought right then and there, 'This kid (Thomas Isabella) is wild.' I wouldn't let the boys play with him but he turned out to be David's best friend."

When asked how he would describe his younger son, David's father responded without hesitation. "Still waters run deep. That's the expression that comes to mind about David. He held a commanding, almost powerful presence. His friends and the people who knew him, well, they knew that and responded to it. It wasn't so much about what he said as who he was." Mark paused, again collecting his thoughts. "I'm proud of both my sons."

"I remember one of the last times I talked with David. He called me one night while he was out with Steven and Trever. He called just to say he was glad he was brought up the way he was. '*It was good for me*' he said. That made me feel good. He told me he was glad he had his faith and no matter what anybody said, he'd never turn it down. It wasn't long after that conversation he was killed."

"'*I would never be afraid to express my faith to anybody.*' David wasn't afraid to tell people about his beliefs. He believed in God, believed Jesus was his savior and wasn't afraid to let anybody know it."

—THE TIMELINE—

"To everything there is a season; a time to every purpose under heaven."

Ecclesiastes 3:1

Quite often, grasping the true meaning of a significant or noteworthy event is difficult to do unless some comparative, parallel occasion can help jog the memory. While it may seem natural to start any story at its' beginning, how relevant would any information from the beginning be if one wasn't even alive to catch it the first time around?

Some might think this young Marine's short time on earth would, in theory, make for a relatively short story about his life. Not so. What follows is a timeline of David's life inclusive of events and various other information regarding events happening in the world at the same time.

There are significant moments in each of our lives; those "Where were you when-?" moments, those "I remember what I was doing the day when—" moments. Some things, of course, are more memorable than others; a few are things we'd assume forget. The world is constantly evolving and becoming a difficult concept to grasp. It's harder still to keep up with all the changes going on in the world around you when you are focused on one event in particular. Time stands still for no one.

01 October 1987 What was it about 1987 that made it a year so worth remembering? For starters, it was the last year that had all different digits (until 2013 rolled around, and ironically enough, the year a biography would be written about David Baker). But there were other notable things that happened that year worth remembering.

Somewhere in Texas, a leaky roof shut down a business for the day. Meanwhile, over in the Midwest, a sales associate was named 'Employee of the Month.' Somewhere up north, a man was arrested for tax evasion. For most people glancing through the papers that October morning, things looked pretty run of the mill; for most people. But in a little town in the Northeastern corner of the Buckeye State, that wasn't the case. That morning in the town of Painesville Ohio, an expectant mother called her doctor because she wasn't feeling well. By the end of that same day at Lake East Hospital about four weeks before he was expected, a baby was brought into the world. Named after his older brother and great-grandfather, little 5lb 12oz David Raymond Baker entered the world.

"He was a quiet little baby, too." Mama B. expressed.

16 October 1990 David's twin sisters were born. "He loved holding the girls."

1991 Operation Desert Storm (AKA 'The Gulf War') began; Freddie Mercury, lead singer of the rock band Queen died; the movie 'Perfect Storm' hit the NE United States 30 October (the same date and area in which 2012's Hurricane Sandy was projected to hit).

1992 Hurricane Andrew hit the U.S.; the first nicotine patch was invented; debuts of the blockbuster movies Backdraft and Thelma and Louise hit theaters everywhere.

19 April 1993 Controversial standoff in Waco, Texas between Branch Davidians and the FBI which resulted in the deaths of 23 children and 53 adults; [11] Brady Bill was introduced; First World Trade Center bombing occurred.

19 April 1995 168 people killed in bombing in Oklahoma City

1998 "Sometime around fourth grade, David brought home a paper, something about career day. It asked, 'What do you want to be when you grow up?' David's answer? A Marine." (M.Baker, Sr.)

1999 Columbine Massacre, JFK, Jr. died in plane crash on east coast

11 September 2001 9-11, World Trade Center Attack, (Pentagon, DC, etc.) "Our second day of infamy.")

—PAINTING A PICTURE—
DAVID RAYMOND BAKER, USMC

"I can do all things through Christ which strengtheth me."

Philippians 4:13

JonBenet Ramsey (25 December 1996), Columbine High School, Colorado (20 April 1999), and September 11th. 2001. What do each of these topics in common? A future Marine. Keeping in mind his age at the time each of these events occurred, David Baker was a young man who possessed particular emotions that seem lacking in today's current, crazy world; compassion and empathy. Webster's dictionary defines empathy as: "The action of understanding, being aware of, being sensitive to, and experiencing feelings and thoughts of another from either the past or present."

JonBenet was the little girl who, after first being reported as missing was later found murdered in her own home in Colorado Christmas Day of 1996. The world eventually learned the little girl had been struck on the back of the head and strangled to death. Several years following the Ramsey incident, Colorado was once again in the news; Columbine. Who could forget the horrific shootings that took place at Colorado's' Columbine High School in April of 1999? Twelve students and a teacher were murdered by two disturbed students brandishing guns and twenty-one more were injured. Then, a little over two years later, 9-11 happened.

The Nation and the world had their own feelings about the events that transpired that morning; and so did a little boy in Ohio. Speaking with Baker's mother, when asked how she felt different events may have shaped him into who he ultimately became; Mama B. revealed how David reacted to those three particular events being reported on the news.

"You know that little girl, the little beauty pageant girl killed in Colorado? JonBenet Ramsey? Her death really affected David. He was so sad. He couldn't believe somebody would do that to a little girl." Mama B. paused in reflection, slowly nodding her head. "It was almost as if he knew her, he was so upset over it."

Mark Sr. also elaborated on the effect JonBenet had on his young son.

"David was young, but even then, his waters ran deep. When all that was going on, he'd cry. '*How could they do that to that little girl?*' He was only 8-years-old but was very sensitive to other people's needs. David was the kind of kid everybody noticed without him having to say a word. He had a 'live and let live' attitude."

Three years later, Colorado produced the Columbine High School Massacre.

Once more, David's mother went into detail. "Columbine happened and I remember David being so worried. Those shootings occurred as he was leaving eighth grade at Our Shepherd, his parochial school and going into ninth grade over at John R. Williams, the public school with Riverside. What happened at Columbine bothered him. I mean, he took it so personally. He felt bad, not understanding how or why students would do that to one another. Even if those two kids had been bullied... (At the time, David couldn't grasp why or how individuals would do that to each other, either.) I remember him asking, '*Mom? What if something like that happens at my new school? I won't know where to go to get away.*' I assured him, "Just be sure you're nice to everyone." I remember telling him, "If someone is being bullied, go stick up for them, say something nice to them. That kind act might change their whole outlook about things later on. You might be the one to change their view of the world, might even make them smile. You might be that guy they think of when they realize everyone isn't so cruel.' He said, '*OK, Mama. I will.*' Clearly he did because of what that one girl told us at his funeral. David always respected the feelings and dignity of others."

Mama B. relayed another story. "I don't remember much from that time but one thing that I do was this girl who'd attended school with David. She'd stood in the line at the funeral home for about five hours. She approached me and said, 'I wanted to tell you something about David. I didn't have many friends at Riverside but David would always say hello or say something nice to me. Your son was so nice. He didn't care what other kids thought."

In the next breath, Mama B. added one more affecting event. "And 9-11. His exact words to me after everything took place that day were, '*Ma, I'm going. I don't want what happened during 9-11 to happen again. I want to be the best of the best.*'"

"And he was." Baker's sister Lauren interjected.

"He told me, '*Mom, I don't want you to be afraid like that.*' I'd have to say that 9-11 was the biggest turning point for him."

Do you think David's made a significant impact on anybody else's life? (An immediate chorus of 'yes!')

Taylor: "I think it took the ultimate sacrifice for people to realize how big of an impact he ultimately made on their lives."

Mark: "It was sooner for some people, though." Mark interjected quietly. "One minute he was here and the next, he wasn't. That's when people realized."

Lauren: "You're right. I don't think people realized," Baker's sister paused as her eyes swelled with tears. "—until he was gone. He wasn't just a good big brother. He was a great guy all the way around."

2002 David graduated from Our Shepherd Lutheran Church Parochial School. At graduation, David was heard to have stated that he wanted to be a Marine, but according to Mama B., "He didn't talk about it much after that."

2003 President George W. Bush announced war against Iraq would begin

2004 David's older brother Mark graduated high school

2005 David enlisted in the Marine's delayed entry program. One week before Thanksgiving, Mike Hatton, a Marine with multiple deployments under his belt, was a speaker at David's school. That day, David came home and informed his family, *"I'm going to be a Marine. I'm taking the ASVAB test (armed services vocational aptitude battery) and doing my physical on Friday."* Mama B. asked her son, "Why the Marines?"

and David responded, '*I want to be the best of the best and that's what the Marines are; the world's best and that's me.*' Mama B. told her youngest son that enlisting was a big step, "But if that's what you want, I'll support you 110%." That Friday came and David did what he had to do. I remember him coming home and saying, '*I leave July 31, 2006.*' I cried," said Mama B. "Pride filled my entire being but fear hit me at the same time and I developed an instant migraine."

2006 June David graduated Riverside High School, Painesville Ohio.

2006 July David and best friend Thomas drove to Indianhead, Maryland to see David's brother Mark who was stationed at the Navy Base there. Originally scheduled to leave for basic training 31 July 2006, David shipped out 01 August instead.

27 October 2007 David completed Marine basic training at Parris Island

24 November 2007 Thanksgiving Day

28 December 2008 Family Portrait
"The kids were all home on leave at the same time. It was the first Christmas I had with the four of them together in a longtime. I'd begged David to bring home his uniform, begged Mark to bring his because I wanted to have a family portrait done. Mark refused but David and Lauren brought theirs. We'd planned doing this portrait because I didn't know when would be the next time would be that I'd have all my kids together."

"I want to say it was the morning of December 27th or the 28th; David walked into my room and says, '*Ma. I've got to talk to you.*' That got my attention. '*What are you going to do with me when I die?*' I told him I was going to stick him in a pickle jar and put him on a shelf. '*No, Ma. What are you going to do?*' When I realized he was being serious, without hesitation I told him we would bury him at Arlington. 'We'll have a service for you here and you'll be buried at Arlington.' He thought about that a moment then asked, '*Why Mama? Don't you want to come see me?*' I kind of looked at him standing there. 'It's not that we wouldn't want to see you. We'd bury you in Arlington because not just anybody gets to be buried there. It's an honorable place to be. It's sacred. But I'll do whatever you want me to do, Honey. You think about it.' All he said was '*OK*' and walked out of the room."

"He came right back in and said, '*OK Mom. That's what we'll do.*' He seemed satisfied with the answer and that was how we planned his funeral. It was totally out of the blue but David had told me all along he wasn't coming home. He was really stuck on that, too. He'd go on and on about what we would do if he'd ever lost a leg or an arm that, he was so convinced; he was so sure he was going to lose something. And David loved wearing flip-flops. First, he was worried about having to get a prosthesis and started talking about flip-flops falling off his fake leg. '*How would I even know if it fell off?*' I told him we'd stick it back on with some Superglue and he goes, '*OK Mom. That's what we'll do.*'"

22 May 2009 David deployed to Afghanistan Memorial Day Weekend, from Bangor, Maine. Bangor was the last stop on U.S. soil for many Marines being deployed overseas. The 1/5 arrived there the Friday before Memorial Day. David called home many times that day, calling everybody because he didn't know when he'd be able to contact anyone again as his cell phone was being shut off the next day. He kept calling and told Mama B., *"Mom, these people are taking my picture."* He wanted her to look up a couple of websites. (Maine) (These organizations used to take pictures of every military person arriving/departing for/from deployment and posted those photographs for the families left behind. However, because of security concerns, they stopped this practice.) [17]

13, 24 June 2009 Mama B. shared several letters David had sent home dated during this time. He'd written, *"If something bad happens—"* making reference to this several times. *"Not nervous yet, but I have bad feelings…"*

24 September 2009 This was the last time David spoke with Mama B. As she relayed the story of that call, she described how he'd told her he was laying up on top of a 7-ton (large truck) while they were talking. Their conversation centered on his homecoming. "I had a special dinner all planned. I was going to make his favorite meal; fried pork chops, mashed potatoes, corn, mac and cheese and enough deviled eggs just for him," Keeping her emotions in check, Mama B. continued, "—with a steak for the next day. He told me he was planning on going to school after he came home for good in November, the paperwork he was going to have to get done—" She shared how she'd told David she had prepared all his paperwork and had it ready to fill out so he could start school immediately. "I'd highlighted everything, you know, laid everything out for him. I'd picked up all the things he needed, fixed all his papers so he could get everything filled out and start school on his G.I. Bill. I told him, 'David, all you'll need to do,'" Mama

B. paused to regain her composure. "We talked about a lot of things that night."

It was this same moment when David's brother Mark began describing the last time he'd spoke with his brother. "It was weird. I mean, when he called, we ended up talking for hours. But we didn't talk. I mean, it was like he was using me as Directory Assistance. He would call and say, '*Dude, give me So-and-So's number.*' I'd give him the number and he'd start repeating it over and over until he hung up and called whoever he was calling. A little while later, he'd call and ask for another number. It went on like that; over and over. He was calling everybody that night." Mark paused reflectively before continuing. "You know, in other conversations we had, he'd tell me all sorts of stuff (about Afghanistan) He'd be like, '*This place sucks. Who the hell would fight over this land?*'"

20 October 2009 LCpl. David Baker killed by IED while walking point on foot patrol.

> "*Taking 'point' means you're the lead soldier of a patrol, the first guy who guides the rest of the unit through enemy terrain. The point man walks ahead, scanning for danger. It is the most exposed position in a war zone. Taking point guarantees you'll be first to wander into an ambush, first to tread on a hidden bomb, first to be framed in the sights of an opposing sniper. Those who take point accept a vastly reduced chance of surviving. Men can 'take point', 'walk point', 'do point', 'be point', but it all amounts to the same thing: high risk.*" [29]

October 2009 was, to that point in time, one of the bloodiest months for U.S. troops. Fifty-seven men and 1 woman were killed.[25] apparently, people don't comprehend what happens during war unless it affects them personally, but by the end of this week in Painesville Ohio, thousands not only realized but would acknowledge the death of one of their own. After a breathtakingly large service held in his native Painesville, Ohio, Baker was buried with full military honors in Arlington National Cemetery, Arlington, Virginia on 04 November, 2009.

Mama B.: "David had told me if anything ever happened to him, there was one particular staff sergeant that he wanted to have come to the house; Staff Sergeant Rivera, a recruiter, was an awesome guy," Mama B. paused. "So I told David he had to put that instruction in with all his paperwork. He'd told me he hadn't had time to change all of that but he wanted someone who KNEW him to come to our door if anything were to happen. That was a big issue for him. What's bizarre is that the week before he was killed, I was sitting at work wondering, 'If your Marine gets killed, how do they tell you? Do they come to your work? Do they send the police to come get you and take you home? Do they come to your work and take you into the office?' Then it was like, Bam! I found out exactly how they do it." When asked when she was told about David's death, Mama B. answered immediately. "They notified me that same day."

"Lauren had called work and told me there was an emergency at home. I asked what the emergency was and all she'd say was, 'You need to come home.' It was a pretty day so I figured she wanted me to come home and have us go do something. I found my boss, told him there was an emergency and I had to go. In seconds, it hit me; 'Not David, not my David!' I started running for the car, screaming, 'Not David! Not David!' I mean, I was driving over curbs and sidewalks, running red lights, driving 100mph screaming, 'Not David' all the way."

"I hit our road and noticed Taylor running from the bowling alley (where she worked at the time). The alley was located on the same road our house was on. So I picked her up and noticed right away she'd been crying. I asked her what was wrong. About three seconds later I was like, 'Oh my God.'"

Mama B. stopped to gather her thoughts. "We got to the house and pulled into the driveway and nothing looked out of the ordinary. Then I walked inside and saw all those Marines in my living room."

Mama B. glanced around the table at each of her kids. "I remember coming through the door immediately saying my name, telling them my name, 'I'm LCpl. David Baker's Mom' because David had told me, *The Marines will come and the first question they're going to ask is if you're my mom.* I felt so bad for all of you because you already knew. Those Marines were standing here but wouldn't tell you anything, they couldn't say..." Her voice trailed off.

—THE CALL—

"Before they call I will answer; and while they are yet speaking, I will hear."

Isaiah 65:24

It was a beautiful fall day in October 2009. Bakers' twin sisters were at home wiling away time goofing and joking around in the living room while waiting for UPS to make a delivery. It being such a nice day, the girls left the front door wide open. It wasn't long before the UPS man came knocking on the door, delivering the neighbor's parcel and was on his way.

The way the living room had been arranged at the time, an entertainment center with a glass front faced the door. The girls were still horsing around in the living room when they noticed they were about to have company. From the reflection off the glass on the entertainment center, Lauren and Taylor noticed a group of people walking up to their door. At first, they thought it was the UPS man coming back for something. Instead, it was a group of Marines dressed in alphas.

"Is Laurie Lewkowski here?" one Marine asked.

"No, she's at work, but you can tell us anything you need to say." One of the girls stated. Of course, the Marines didn't say another word. They didn't have to say a word. The girls knew.

"It was the worst of the worst when they showed up. They didn't have to say anything. Their body language said it all."

"I was immediately on the phone calling Mom when one of them finally spoke. 'Don't tell her we're here. Don't put her into a panic.' It was like they were reading off some report or script or something. They never faltered, never wavered. Not once; just stuck to the script."

Mama B.: "When the girls called, I was like, 'Oh my God! Not David!' I hit the door running. I was going through red lights and stop signs, running over the berms along the side—" She paused abruptly. "As soon as I pulled into the driveway, I still didn't know what was up; just assumed. I ran into the house and saw four or five Marines (I don't remember how many there were) and automatically started telling them my name. 'I'm Laurie Lewkowski' because David had told me that'd be the first thing they'd ask if they ever had to come to the house."

"Are you the mother of Lance Corporal David R. Baker?"

"The CACO (casualty assistance calls officer) began to read, '*From the United States Marine Corps, and President Barack Obama, we are here to inform you that your son Lance Corporal David R. Baker passed away the 20th of October, 2009.*' At that moment, all I knew was David had been killed, nothing else. They wouldn't tell me anything about what happened."

Taylor: Standing for emphasis, David's sister spoke. "I tried talking with them as calmly and rationally as I could, trying not to cry."

Mama B.: "Another set of CACO's had been sent to Mark Sr's home but I called his work and told him, "Come to the house NOW." He asked why and I told him to get over here. He asked me why again and I said, 'They killed David! They've killed our boy!' He came to the house immediately." Mama B. paused before speaking again, softer this time. "I used to get up around 0445 to get ready for work. David was killed at one-fifteen in the afternoon in Afghanistan. I think with the time difference and everything, he was killed around the same time I got up for work."

Taylor: "Around here, October has turned into a bittersweet month for us. We have so many birthdays and anniversaries... and death to remember."

Mama B.: "Back in August or September, before all this happened, I'd called a local DJ (Hoss from WKKY 104.7 FM) to see if he could help me get a discount or knew of a way to get a cheap flight to California. I wanted to see David when he come in and wanted to be at Camp Pendleton to surprise him. Long story short, Hoss, helped raise money for a plane ticket to get me out there but David was KIA before he got to come home. After what happened, I didn't want people to think bad things about donating money so I had a friend call Hoss and tell him to return all the donations." She paused before continuing. "Hoss came to David's funeral. I ran to him when I saw him." Mama B. teared up as she recalled the day. "After news of David's passing got out, people still kept sending money. Hoss gave me an envelope full at the funeral which we ended up donating. I remember waves of people that day but don't recall much else." Looking at each of her kids, Mama B. turned apologetic. "And I felt so bad because I wasn't there for my other kids. I was like Jell-O." Her voice trailed again as she replayed the events of that day in her mind. "There're certain things I'll never forget, but that day was..."

Taylor: "David was just one person, but he touched so many lives. Painesville isn't a well-known place on the map. Considering where he was from, I think David inspired and touched so many lives."

21 October 2009 Family flew to Dover, Delaware to receive David

29 October 2009 Family went to Cleveland-Hopkins Airport to meet some of David's Marine Corps Brothers who had flown in to be pall bearers.

30 October 2009 Calling hours held in Painesville for David.

31 October 2009 The Funeral Procession: David's procession disembarked upon Ohio's Interstate-90 from Vrooman Road. The procession took Route 84 to Riverside Drive and went past his high school to the church where his services were held. It was here that Mama B. received David's Purple Heart. (Incidentally, his service was held at the same church where David attended parochial school.)

01 November 2009 Family left for Arlington National Cemetery, Arlington, Va.

With both your brothers being Marines, did either of you ever imagine you'd get that knock at the door?

Taylor: "No. But it happened. The Marines didn't come right out and say anything. I mean, they couldn't. But as soon as Lauren and I figured it out, I started yelling at them. I was yelling at Marines, 'Just go!' I'd told Lauren 'They're the bad guys. They need to leave.' I actually told all of them that, too. 'You need to leave.' I was mad and kept telling them to get out, to leave."

Lauren: "I was worried about everybody else. I was worried for Mom, for Taylor, and Mark. I mean, I was worried about Mark. Despite everything we were all going through at the time, none of us were talking to each other.

Taylor: The day we found out, when Markie came home, I mean he's never been a real huggie kind of guy when it comes to his sisters, but he came home and gave me the biggest hug he's ever given to me. From that point on, everything was awful. After the Marines came to the house, I went out into the yard and screamed. I remember one of our neighbors came outside and asked what happened. At first, I just stood there. I mean, I couldn't say anything. Then I started waving my arms like, 'Strike three, you're out' and finally told her what was wrong. 'David. David is dead.' She handed me her phone. That's how I started telling friends of the family. I remember having to tell all David's friends. I was the one who told Thomas (Isabella)."

"One day before David was killed, Thomas and I had been standing around at school hanging out and talking. I remember telling him David was going to be home soon and how excited I was and had plans to do so many things when he got back. But then we got the news. I had to tell Thomas. He was a total wreck. Thomas was another one of David's 'boys'. It was awful. He took it so hard. A couple weeks after everything happened, I'd gotten upset at school because somebody had said something about David, about the way he died. I happened to see Thomas right after that. I was crying so hard and he freaked out. He got all up in the guy's face and freaked out about David."

When was the last time either of you spoke to David?

In unison: "High school graduation."

Taylor: "No, actually, he called after that in September (2009) and asked how everything was going. That conversation didn't seem any different." She leaned back in her chair. "About six months before David died, I'd had a dream that it had actually happened. I woke up upset and told my friend about it. I almost felt guilty, like maybe if I'd told him about that dream, he wouldn't have been killed."

Lauren: "I think that was the last time I spoke to him as well." Baker's sister paused before continuing. "When he died, it wasn't about feeling one way or another." Lauren paused in reverie. "About a week after David died, I saw him in a dream. It was so real. He was at a window and was wearing an orange shirt and a backpack. I was like, 'Oh my God. It's David. David's here' then Mark started getting upset and David said, '*I know I'm gone. I know I died but I'm ok. You're ok and everything is going to be ok.*' I woke up crying.' Lauren stopped again. "I remember thinking, 'How do you know when you're dead? Can you come back to tell the people you love that you know? It was actually a good dream, because David said he was ok."

Mama B.: "I have these dreams. One of them is in Key West. David receives a bill in the mail stating he owes a lot of money. So I'm trying to find this Marine base to tell him about this piece of mail. In this dream, I can remember a high fence and a lot of Marines all around." Mama B. took a slow breath before continuing. "So I get there and am like, 'David, you don't have to go. You don't have to go. They're not gonna let you go.' And he says, '*I hear you Ma. Ma, I'm ok.*' I keep telling him 'they're not gonna let you go' and he says, '*Ma, I'm ok. Ma, I'm ok*' but I can't see him. He hears me though and he's gotten my message that he doesn't have to deploy. It's the only dream I've ever had that wasn't one of my regular nightmares."

02 November 2009 Memorial Service in Ohio

"If one part suffers, all parts suffer with it. And if one part is honored, all the parts are glad." I Corinthians 12:21 as spoken by Pastor Jim Weaver, First Baptist Church. "David became a difference maker. 'Send me. I will go.' David answered a call to serve and became a US Marine. Ronald Reagan once said, 'Some people spend their entire lives wondering if they made a difference. Marines don't have that problem.' Neither did David."

"From the Cleveland Hopkins International Airport, the family of LCpl. Baker was escorted by hundreds of members of the Leathernecks Nation, Freedom Riders, Blue Knights, and Axemen motorcycle clubs to deliver David's body to the funeral home in Eastlake, Ohio." [8]

If any portion of a person's life could be measured by the number of people present at one's funeral, than David's too brief 22 years could easily have represented the entire lifetime of several men. The number of people present to see this young Marine off measured literally into the thousands. There were over one hundred vehicles in his funeral procession alone, never mind the accompanying motorcycles. (As for the motorcycle clubs, there were PGR (Patriot Guard Riders), Leathernecks, Copperheads, Axemen, and Hell's Angels to name a few). This Marine's initial memorial service was held at the Zion Lutheran Church in Mentor, Ohio.

American flags, Marine flags and absolute droves of people lined both sides of the road for as far as the eyes could see. Shoulder to shoulder it seemed, there were no gaps or spaces to be observed. Motorcycles parked in rows the length of the roadway and the leaves of autumn scattered on the ground. Blue sky and sunshine belied the emotion below. The black hearse arrived and the Marines snapped to attention. Onlookers watched in hushed silence as the silver, flag-draped casket was carried into the church.

When services concluded, the same sky hung overhead with the same sun shining down on the masses. The scene greeting those exiting the church was no different from what they witnessed on their way in. There were fire trucks, motorcycles, police cars, and more people lining the streets; waiting to pay tribute to a Marine they all felt they knew.

The service at Mt. Zion was not to mark the completion of this Marine's journey. David's voyage was by no means final. The hallowed grounds of Confederate General Robert E. Lee's former family home in Virginia would be Lance Corporal David R. Baker's final resting place; a place called Arlington.

Mama B.: "That church from out west (whose name shall go without mention) had plans to be in Painesville." Mama B. paused. "I guess they did come with every intention of protesting David's funeral. They were all I could think about during his service; that when we come out, those people were going to be standing outside waiting."

Taylor: "I wasn't afraid of them. I'd have probably been arrested for assault. I was almost hoping they'd be out there. I mean, they planned to come to my brother's funeral and protest because 'God loves dead soldiers?' They wanted to tell me my brother deserved to die? Just who the hell do those people think they are? I'd have had no trouble telling them about how David died defending their right to come here and say the things they thought they were in need of saying. But to actually plan to come here and protest his funeral specifically?

That would've been the worst thing they could have done. And you know, they were here. I heard they were afraid after they got up here and saw all the people. They better damn sure have been afraid for their lives."

Mama B.: (Interjecting) "Apparently, that group rarely comes to Northern Ohio, but as I mentioned, they did come." She paused. "Those people planned to protest. I was so anxious, so worried they'd be outside." Mama B. paused a moment. "The disc jockey from WMMS Rock 100.7, Rover, had somehow gotten wind of their plans. While he was on air, he asked everybody to turn their car stereos up loud so we wouldn't have to hear them (that gutless church from Kansas). And everybody did it. We didn't know this was going on until one of Lauren's friends heard about it on the radio. Of course, she called Lauren and Lauren called me in the funeral limo during our drive to Vrooman Road, Riverside and Zion (the Church). We had the driver turn the radio to 100.7 and you could hear Zac Brown's '*Chicken Fried*' throughout the drive. Rover played that song for hours that day. But once we stopped and all of us stepped off the bus, it was so quiet outside. There were thousands of people standing out there, everywhere you looked, yet all you could hear was the sound of flags flapping in the wind."

Originally posted 07 November 2009 by Fox News, the following was a news article retrieved from the Internet October of 2012 entitled, '*For Marines in Afghanistan; IED's are a Constant Fear.*' [28]

There are few songs as mournful and haunting as Taps played for a fallen warrior, and on an isolated combat outpost (COP) in southern Afghanistan it has been sounded for David Baker, a 22-year-old Marine lance corporal who was six weeks short of going home when he was killed in an explosion.

"He was on a hill next to this village," said Sgt. David Hine, of Weapons Company, 1st Battalion, 5th Marines. "Everyone was in single file behind him. He'd just unfolded his (metal) detector and taken a step..."

Baker, a mine sweeper, was killed outright by an estimated 50 pounds of homemade explosives buried beneath sand and detonated by a pressure plate.

"It was typical of the IEDs we find here," said Sgt. Grey Jewett, an explosive ordnance disposal expert attached to Weapons Company's 81 Platoon. "They're mostly pressure-plate activated, with 50-pound charges. [The Taliban are] trying to disrupt our supply routes and piss us off—and we are."

IEDs are the Taliban's weapon of choice in the Nawa District of southern Helmand Province, about 50 miles from Pakistan. The total area of the district, which according to one Marine was "the home of the boogeyman" when they arrived during the summer, is a bit over 400 square miles. Weapons Company's area of operation, nicknamed AO Dixie, is about 91 square miles of desert with a large swath of farming villages located along irrigation canals near the Helmand River.

Marines in the district have established more than 20 outposts around those communities to guard against dislodged Taliban returning from the neighboring district of Marjah, about 3 miles away and without any American presence.

During earlier clearing operations it was estimated that as many as 500 Taliban gunmen were in Nawa. The number is now smaller, but hard to put a figure on.

"It's all a guess at this point," said a senior officer with Task Force Leatherneck, which is in charge of Marine units in Helmand. "Numbers range between 50 and 150 and from 10 to 50—all in the same location.

First Lt. Clint Hall was in charge of Combat Outpost Sullivan, which anchors Marine efforts in AO Dixie. He believes there are about 30 Taliban in his zone, but "that fluctuates, and more and more people who at one time had ties (to the Taliban) have turned over a new leaf and use their shovel now for farming instead of planting IEDs."

But IEDs are being planted nonetheless. And while the number has dropped 75 percent from the summer, discovering five a week is not uncommon, Hall said.

According to Sgt. Jewett and Staff Sgt. Matthew Grant, leader of the EOD team whose job it is to defuse and destroy IEDs, three types of mines are used in Nawa: the pressure-plate anti-vehicle IED, the directional fragmentation charge (a home-made Claymore anti-personnel mine), and "pulled" mines. Both the fragmentation IED and anti-vehicle pull mine use a plastic water or soda bottle filled with material as the detonation initiator for a larger charge. They're set off using of piece of string or cord pulled through the bottle to connect metal parts to complete an electrical detonation circuit by an insurgent hiding several hundred yards away.

Unlike Iraq, where IEDs first gained prominence, the explosives used in Nawa are not conventional ordnance, such as mortars and artillery shells. Instead, they're made from ammonium nitrate used in fertilizer.

"They're good at disguising it. They take their time planting it and put it in (the ground) well."

Jewett and Grant repeatedly encourage Marines about what to watch for when patrolling the desert or around villages: kite string or any type of cord, freshly turned earth, collections of rocks, clumps of brush, plastic jugs and coffee cans.

Two days after a memorial service for Baker at Combat Outpost Sullivan, Marines returned to the village of Korkoran. Their target was an empty mud-and-brick house on its edge from where potshots are sometimes taken at patrols. It was next to "Baker's Hill," where the Marine from Ohio was killed.

"Gone but not forgotten," a Marine wrote on his helmet about Lance Corporal Baker. With redeployment nearing, the Marines of Weapons Company are hoping Taps won't be sounded here again. Ibid.

Many are maimed or killed by these devices; but IED's also produced another casualty; desensitization. If people read or hear about a particular topic with enough frequency, pretty soon no matter what the issue is about, it becomes a matter of little consequence. Nobody is held specifically accountable for the deaths of those killed by these devices, except perhaps to say in the broadest term possible, "insurgents, Taliban, Afghanis" No SWAT gets called; no BOLO's put out. Murdered; most without justice, all in the line of duty, fighting for their country.

03 November 2009 "He Made It to Arlington" Following a funeral befitting a hero in his hometown of Painesville, Marine Lance Corporal David Baker was laid to rest in Arlington National Cemetery with full military honors; Section 60, Site 8856.

29 November 2009 Date LCpl. Baker was to have completed combat duty

14 December 2009 David's unit returned stateside.

05 February 2010 Roll Call, Camp Pendleton California

26 November 2011 Honor and Remember Flag Ceremony, Riverside High School, Painesville Ohio

29 November 2011 129th General Assembly Joint Session; Statehouse, Columbus Ohio: Senator John Eklund presented Baker's family David's Ohio Military Medal of Distinction, and resolution. (David was the only one who received a resolution that day.)

From a copy of the Senate Resolution #154 adopted by the state of Ohio on 28 November 2011 as presented by Senator John Eklund, "In memory of David Raymond Baker" and reads as follows:

Members of the Senate of the 129th General Assembly of Ohio extend posthumous recognition to Lance Corporal David Raymond Baker as the recipient of the Ohio Military Medal of Distinction, and Whereas David Baker was truly a remarkable individual, for the combined courage and dedication with tremendous strength and resolve during his loyal service with the United States Marine Corps. A 2006 graduate of Riverside High School, he was assigned to the 1st Battalion, 5th Marines, 1st Marine Division, I Marine Expeditionary Force, and was serving as a motorman in Afghanistan when he was killed in the line of duty. This prestigious honor is indeed, a fitting tribute to him, and it is only appropriate that we commend him as a patriotic and hard-working American—"

The ultimate sacrifice he made to defend the ideals of democracy will stand as a monument to his personal character; and the world is a better place for his having been in it."

04 August 2012 Ohio Veteran's Memorial Park (www. ovmp.org) Memorial Service, Clinton, Ohio: David's name is one of hundreds inscribed and memorialized on the wall in Clinton, Ohio.

Mama B.: "I'd never heard of the Memorial Park until a local Leatherneck said something about it. This Marine came to me the Friday before and asked if I wanted to go to the Park. I said sure. I mean, at that point, I didn't know if David's name was already on it or not. So we went all the way out there. It was a big rush and we arrived barely five minutes before the whole thing started." She paused as she collected her memories from that day. "The first thing I remember was that they were handing out beautiful yellow roses to the Gold Star mothers. And you know, for things like this, I'm not one to stand up and get anything. I mean, I was wearing David's memorial shirt and I was there but, well…the Leatherneck who'd mentioned the service in the first place was there as well and he motioned to the folks, telling them, 'You have a Gold Star Mom right here.' So they brought me a rose, because I wasn't going to go up and get it." Mama B. paused, becoming tearful. "I didn't want anybody to think, I mean, you know, I didn't care if I got one or not. I wasn't there for the rose; I wasn't there to be known or seen. I was there because I wanted to see David's name." She took a deep breath before continuing.

"So they gave me my rose, and we listened to the speakers. I remember it was, really hot, that afternoon." Mama B.'s voice grew hushed "I was sitting in the back of the crowd there. I didn't want to be in the front. I didn't want that. But as soon as they unveiled that section on the memorial, I went bursting through. Pam Staff went with me. All the Leathernecks that were with us made sure we got up to the wall and the Afghanistan panel; then I saw David's name."

"They did some Honor and Remember presentations that day too, but I don't remember a whole lot of that because I was still computing everything. You know, taking in the fact David's name was on this enormous wall." Mama B. paused once again, emotion thick in the air. "I wanted his name there, but I didn't. That was real. I mean, stuff like that, I appreciate what they do, why they put their names up there but it's like I draw a blank." Mama B. hesitated before continuing "I don't remember a lot. It's like everything is still. David's name is there, Titus Reynolds's Kevin Cornelius's…"

Sisters: "It's like at Arlington. We go, we see our brother's name on his headstone there and it's like, we know he's," they hesitated; "—not here with us. To see his name like that, so detached. It's like a missing link."

October 2012—The Cedar Chest—

After David died, all his effects were shipped home. Mama B. bought a Lane Cedar chest to store everything in.

"I wasn't about to leave all his belongings in those boxes."

Sorting through that cedar chest were items that defined David Baker's life in great detail. As well as might be expected, there were sets of BDU's (battle dress uniform), numerous pictures, books, clothes, ditty bags, his flag, as well as two red, velveteen bags; personal effects of David's. Collectively, these things were acknowledgements of the life that was this Marine's There were belongings but there were also letters; scores and scores of letters and cards of sympathy and concern.

Among the collection of envelopes and cards were letters from a variety of notable individuals which included correspondence from General Stanley McChrystal, (retired Army General, former commander of the International Security Assistance Force (ISAF) and U.S. Forces in Afghanistan), George Voinovich, (former senator of Ohio). A letter from L.D. Nicholson, (Brigadier General of the USMC) graced the collection of correspondence as well.

From a letter dated 12 November 2009: Admiral M.G. Mullen: 17th Chairman of the Joint Chiefs of Staff, principal military advisor to the President, et al. sworn to post October 2007:

"We do not like to think about it, but we ask them to risk their lives. And they do so, repeatedly, unhesitatingly. David answered that call, sacrificing his life to make better and more free the lives of millions of people he did not know, in a place he did not live. He served nobly his Marine Corps, his country, and the cause of liberty."

From a letter dated 20 November 2009: J. T. Conway, General USMC/Commandant of the Marines:
"David earned a reputation as an outstanding Marine and an even finer person. His integrity was beyond reproach and his selfless leadership an inspiration to many."

—NOT ONLY HIS MOTHER'S HEART—

"*The father of a righteous child has great joy; a man who fathers a wise son rejoices in him.*"
                                        —Proverbs 23:24

"I'm flattered and honored that somebody wanted to do this for David. But it's still hard to talk about. David was the kind of guy, I mean, I don't know how to explain it. What David had, you can't teach. It was a gift from God."
                    David's Father Mark Baker, Sr.

" *'We've got a job to do, and now we're going to go do it.'* Before David deployed, he'd told me he felt that if he got sent to Afghanistan, he wouldn't be coming back. I honestly believe David knew he wasn't coming home. As a parent, you assure your kids, you tell them not to worry, that everything is going to be okay." Mr. Baker's voice turned reflective. "You know, he was on the homestretch when he was killed, due home the following month." Expressing an audible sigh, he questioned, "Why did a kid who was so sweet, so loving, so loved have to have this happen to him?"

The character of the conversation changed as Mark Sr. started speaking once more. His voice was a little softer, a little sadder.

"The Marine's came to our house. Laurie had called but wouldn't detail anything over the phone. She only said I had to get to the house immediately." Mark paused in thought. "I mean, I can't remember leaving my building at work. I think that was the last time I worked for probably three months. All the 'what ifs', the guilt I had. You automatically go into 'Why? Why? Why?' I remember thinking Laurie had to have made a mistake. But when I got home, there were Marines everywhere."

"It was a big, huge, huge deal around here (Painesville) when David passed away. They shut the freeway down. The response from the community was so overpowering. It was so very overwhelming. I mean, I'm saying this on top of losing a child, which is indescribably overwhelming in itself. It's not something that makes a whole lot of sense to me." David's father spoke frankly. "Trust me. I was mad at God for a while, and in some ways I guess I still am. But it's not about me, is it? If I think about what I tried to teach the boys as they were growing up, David's absolutely where he needed to be."

"At his service in Ohio, there was an unbelievable line of people outside the funeral home. The director wanted us to speed things up because it was getting very late. I was thinking, 'What? These people have been standing in line for three hours waiting to pay respect to my son.' I mean, that's how many people there were.

"There was one girl who came; she told us she felt she had to come see David. She professed not to be very popular; the kind of kid who got made fun of a lot. She came so she could tell us how David would always say hello to her and smile. That's what my kid was all about. He was real. Nothing phoney about him."

"Funeral services were held in Painesville at David's parochial school/church. The church was packed; perhaps a thousand people inside with absolute thousands outside. To this day, I can't begin to tell you the feeling I had regarding the community's response to his death. It was," Mr. Baker paused in reflection. "From the time he got home, it was so hard for me to deal with. All the news stations were at his calling hours; I had my brothers do the interviews." Mark's voice turned melancholy. "There was so much love for David." The phone grew silent, then in a softer voice, Mark Baker, Sr. reiterated, "People came out of the woodwork. There was such a tremendous show of love and respect for my kid. That's when I started feeling honored and privileged to be his father." Big Mark wasn't finished with his thought yet. "The world gets smaller as you get older."

"A local radio station found out about that church from out west and their plans to come protest David's funeral. All that bunch did was draw more attention to David, though I doubt that was their intention. They pulled everybody together up here. There were so many law enforcement personnel waiting. It was something to see; indescribable. It's still overwhelming to me. I don't know what drove thousands of people to come line the roads and wave flags for David. It's unbelievable to me that people would come to stand outside to watch a car go by. For me to see how people felt made me feel honored and humbled." Mark Baker grew silent in thought. "He was a good kid. He was a good son."

"I remember him sitting down here one night and saying; 'This is what I want to do' He was looking for my support. So I told him, 'you're gonna get through it.' I think of all the times he would call and we'd talk. He knew he wasn't coming back. And you know something else? Taking point, David led over a hundred foot patrols over there; one hundred patrols to his credit. That's a lot for one guy. Apparently, his reigning officer thought so, too."

"There was a retired officer, a liaison between the U.S. Forces and the local villages in Afghanistan. David was assigned to his security detail. Apparently, they'd taken fire someplace and David went out ahead of them and returned fire until they all got back to safety. A few weeks later, David was killed. That retired colonels' wife wrote me a letter which essentially said if it wasn't for David, her husband might not be alive today. David went out and did what he was supposed to do. I thought it was incredible she actually picked up pen and paper to write me a letter about how David saved her husband's life."

Mr. Baker continued answering questions as conversation soon turned to the Memorial Roll Call held at Camp Pendleton. "Ah, the Roll Call." Mark paused briefly. "It was for all the men his unit had lost. For me, it was sort of like the services in Painesville, except for the fact that this one was in California; powerful, emotional. It was very, sad to start connecting with other families who'd lost their sons, so emotional." Mr. Baker paused in recollection. "That whole base knew David. They all knew about him, knew what he stood for. They knew how many lives he had touched." Another thoughtful silence filled the line. "So many people were affected by one tragic moment; connected. Everybody wanted to let us know how much he meant to them."

"I feel God blocks things out on purpose but I still feel guilty that I can't remember some things. Everything went so fast. Every time we turned around, there were people calling, and asking questions. We weren't allowed any time to begin healing." Mr. Baker's voice softened. "You can't cope, can't function. I mean, there was nowhere to turn. It was the worst feeling in the world. And sleep? You can't sleep. You might dream but even the good dreams are horrible because you know he won't be here when you wake up. It gets less, but it never, ever, goes away. Sometimes I worry about people forgetting David." Big Mark was lost in a thought. "When it first happened, I couldn't tell you the thousands of cards we received, from all over the world. Then it stopped. Time marches on, the next story comes up. I don't want anybody to forget him, but the world keeps on turning."

Mama B.: "It was October 29th, the day of David's procession out to Cleveland Hopkins Airport when we went to pick up his body. We'd all gathered at the funeral home." She paused, tears filling her eyes. Taking a slow, deep breathe, she began speaking again. "There were so many bikers out there; Copperheads, Freedom Riders, Blue Knights, Axemen, PGR (Patriot Guard Riders), hundreds of members of the Leatherneck Nation, ordinary people; Lauren. Taylor. Anna. Lisa. (David's sisters). Several bikers had asked the girls if they wanted to ride on the bikes out to the airport. David's death seemed to reunite the family. It was one of the things that I remember so distinctly. It was nice to see that. As we made our way out to Hopkins, every on-ramp from Eastlake was closed all the way to the Airport. Policemen, firemen, regular people; they were all standing out beside their vehicles and saluting us, saluting David."

Lauren: "It was a nice day, weather-wise. When we were in the procession going across I-90, it was so crazy seeing all those people. Like Mom said, there were cops blocking all the ramps, (and they just don't do that) and so many people standing outside their cars. I mean, who the hell gets out of their car like that on a major highway? But all these people were out there saluting, older people especially. You could tell they were upset and sad and not stopping out there just to stop. They knew what our procession was about; they were all paying their respects. That day was surreal, so, wow." Her voice trailed. "I think the only time it got chilly was on the way back from the funeral home. It wasn't because of the weather, either. We were all on the bikes and the day was beautiful." She paused in thought. "My mind was wrapped around David coming home. I mean, it was like, 'My brother's home.' I was sad but excited. My brother was finally home but," David's sister voice softened, "—probably the coldest I've ever felt was on the way back from the airport after we'd picked him up."

Family: "As we our way back, the ramps to I-90-East were still closed. Fire trucks and ambulances were on every overpass and huge, enormous flags were hanging."

By this time, all of David's family had gathered in the kitchen, tearfully relaying their views about that day. "There were all these people standing there with signs, so many of them; everywhere as far as you could see. I had never seen so many people in one place like that before. And it was all for David."

Mama B.: "I'll never forget one man standing along Route 90 with his two little boys. The child in his arms was holding an American flag as high as he could; his little arm was almost hyper-extended. He was in his daddy's arms, waving that flag without knowing why."

Lauren: "The more people I saw, the more I cried. The closer we got to the school, the more people there were. Men, women, children," She paused. "It didn't matter. All those people were crying. And all you saw were people and flags. "

Mama B.: "Even though there were so many people, you could hear the flags whipping in the wind and leaves rustling in the trees," She paused. "It was one of the most peaceful, sad, and quietest moments during that whole time."

Taylor: "Trever came (to Ohio) and told me about what happened to David. I was nervous but remember asking him how he found out. Trever had been at his own post BS'ing with friends when they heard there'd been an explosion. He was squad leader there and tried to contact the people to find out what happened. The way he eventually found out for sure was when he heard, 'The angel is Baker.'"—Long silence. "David always referred to Trever as, '*My Boy Simpson, my Boy Simpson.*' The first time I ever talked to Trever was this one time David called home. For some reason, on that call, they both told me not to date anybody. David went on to advise me not to go to either of the colleges I'd been accepted to. He said, '*Go to Lakeland, instead*' which is where I ended up going."

Lauren: "David always got what he wanted; one way or another."

In the weeks following an emotional gathering at her brother's grave in Arlington in 2013, David's sister Taylor texted the author with another memory to share about her brother.

Taylor: "I'm here at the beach remembering one summer when David was home for a few weeks. It was the summer of junior year; Lauren was away in basic training so it was just him and I. We got up early and went out to breakfast and to go buy him some swim trunks. We went and picked up his friend and all of us went to the beach. We had a blast.

While we were out there swimming, I remember riding on David's back because he wanted to swim really far out. I'm not the strongest swimmer or very tall, for that matter. We went out there just about every day he was home. It was the best two weeks ever."

—THEY WERE ONLY SUPPOSED TO BE YELLOW RIBBONS—

(But They Turned Into a Gold Star)

"The Lord is my strength and my song..."
Psalm 118:14

Mama B.: "When they brought David home from Dover, I didn't want to see him. I mean, they wouldn't let me, anyway. The only people who went were Uncle Matt and Markie. I told Markie (David's brother), 'I'm going to ask you a lot of questions, but the only one I want you to answer is, 'Is it for sure David?' Because of course, I was hoping it wasn't. When Mark came back, I asked him, 'Was it David?' He told me yes. I asked what he looked like and Mark told me, 'Mom, he was perfect. He was perfect.' Mama B. paused to gather her composure.

"I remember getting his official death certificate. David was killed October 2009 but I didn't get the official certificate until July 2010. So I was reading it and it said onset of death was from the blast and was in a matter of seconds. But 'cause of death,'" she paused and looked at the author expectantly. "What do you think it said his cause of death was?" (Fitzgerald had already read through a number of articles that stated an IED as the cause and started to answer when Mama B. quickly held up her hand to quiet her.) "Cause of death was listed as homicide. I mean, I never once thought, it never dawned on me to think my son was murdered. Homicide. I'd never thought about that until I read it in black and white. Then it pissed me off to think that somebody had deliberately murdered him, my child. David was killed; on purpose." Mama B's voice fell silent.

Air Force Mortuary Affairs Center:
LCpl. David R. Baker:
LCpl. David R. Baker's Homecoming; Dover Air Force Base.
(Commentary of Video of David's return to the States.)

With gloved hands, they slowly, resolutely marched to the aircraft in wait on the runway. The Marines who had patiently been waiting in formation along the tarmac slowly approached the steps. Inside, a glimpse of additional Marines; standing fast, unwavering at the side of a flag-draped transfer case through a moment of prayer, readying for the final moment of their brother's homecoming.

Those white-gloved hands slowly raised in unison a somber salute before moving this Marine to the waiting lift. In one coordinated movement, they lifted their brother and carried him forward. As his casket was slowly lowered to the ground, his escort remained at attention. The detail on the ground below slowly stepped forward, moving as one, gently pulling the transfer case and its precious cargo to their grasps.

His flag-draped casket was gently placed into an unmarked, white van. As it unhurriedly pulled away, the detail raised their hands again, in final salute. Blue lights glistened in the distance and the runway turned vacant once more. The van preceded, the detail left behind and another Marine was going home.

—FINAL ROLL CALL—

05 February 2010, Camp Pendleton, California.

"But they that wait upon the LORD shall renew their strength; they shall mount up with wings as eagles; they shall run, and not be weary; and they shall walk, and not faint."

Isaiah 40:31

Speaking with Baker's family in their home a few days after what would have been the lance corporals twenty-fifth birthday, the stories flowed freely, with everybody interjecting and adding details to one another's information as each person took their turn. When conversation progressed to details regarding the memorial ceremony (Roll Call) held at Camp Pendleton, Mama B. quickly made the comment, "Heartbreaking." This was followed by Baker's twin sisters each contributing their thoughts. David's brother spoke at length as well.

Mama B.: "Numbing." (She uttered her opinion quietly from across the table.)

Mark: (David's brother) "I knew it was all real, but that Roll Call was the nail," Mark paused. "I mean at that instant, I was like, 'This shit is real.'" He took a moment to collect his thoughts before continuing. "Actually, I was proud and sad at the same time. I know he died doing something that made sure the rest of them came back."

Trever: "I spoke at the roll call held at Pendleton."

Mark: "Roll call in the Marines is an accountability formation. Everybody's present. For a Memorial Roll Call, they'll usually call off four or five names of people who are actually there, you know, to get things started then they'll start calling out names of the missing. They'll call a name, repeat it two or three times and then ring the bell. The bell is rung for the fallen since they aren't able to speak for themselves."

Trever: "In Afghanistan, they'd start off a Memorial Roll Call by first placing some boxes or sandbags, you know, to set everything else up on. We used sandbags. They had them all lined up and like Mark said, everybody's present. For Memorial Roll Call, there's ceremonial placement of rifles, boots, dog tags for the field cross and then speeches, some prayer and the actual roll call at the end."

"For roll calls in-country, it's obvious war couldn't shut down just so friends of the fallen can attend services. When the Memorial Roll Call was held in Afghanistan, only select Marines were allowed to go. There was still a mission to complete, a job to do. Even though a brother had fallen, the war still went on."

—HIS FAMILY ALWAYS BEFORE HIM—

(And Jesus Had His Back)

"Greater love hath no man than this that he lay down his life for his friends."

John 5:13

It was no secret David was a man of faith. Having attended parochial school throughout the earlier years of his life, David was proud to be so identified with his values. He was never ashamed to admit his faith, either. He didn't preach or try to force those beliefs on people but would not hesitate to defend them as he saw necessary. If somebody blasted his religion, he'd be sure to set them straight. He didn't care what people thought.

In conducting the numerous interviews with family and friends, one particular story stood out. Asked about what kind of man he thought David was, one Marine drove an important point home as he expressed his answer.

"David had a lot of ink (tattoos). He was proud of it all, too. I remember he had the word 'FAMILY' across his abdomen in great big letters, a crucifix on his right shoulder blade and a huge, filigree cross taking up his entire back. So as far as the priorities in life? He'd tell you without any qualms, but you didn't have to be told. You could literally look at him and know what mattered most to him in life. He had that great big tat across his abs saying 'FAMILY' in huge script and on his back, he had his cross. I mean it was huge. It went across his back down to his crack and he had a picture of God on one shoulder. It was like he always had his family before him and you know God had his back."

David Baker's favorite biblical verse was the 23rd Psalm, which incidentally, is called *The Psalm of David.*

The Psalm of David
(Psalm 23: 1-6)

The Lord is my shepherd; I shall not want.
He maketh me to lie down in green pastures:
He leadeth me beside the still waters.
He restoreth my soul:
He leadeth me in the paths of righteousness for his name's sake.
Yea, though I walk through the valley of the shadow of death,
I will fear no evil: for thou art with me;
Thy rod and thy staff they comfort me.
Thou preparest a table before me in the presence of mine enemies:
Thou anointest my head with oil; my cup runneth over.
Surely goodness and mercy shall follow me all the days of my life:
And I will dwell in the house of the LORD forever.

—'PAPA' STEVE GYURE: DAVID BAKER'S GRANDFATHER—

Posted prominently on the diesel truck he drives, David's grandfather has displayed: *"My Grandson Lcpl. David R. Baker gave all. Afghanistan 10-20-09 USMC"*

"I've put this interview off because I didn't know how I was going to put things into words." Mr Gyure's, ('Papa' to David and his siblings) was an elusive interview to catch. He and Fitzgerald already had opportunity to meet each another many months before David's biography actually came into fruition, so Fitzgerald believed Mr. Gyure's interview would be easy to obtain. That wasn't exactly the case.

His interview started at the absolute beginning, with Mr. Gyure being asked how he felt the day David was born. "Happy is all I know to say. You know, as far as his growing up, David was a normal kind of kid. I mean, he was a polite and kind little boy and got into all the normal kinds of mischief you'd expect from a kid, but David was *always* kind of quiet and calm." Mr Gyure took a moment to gather his thoughts before continuing. "Whenever the boys would come to the house, Grandma would take Markie and they'd go do their thing so me and David would go do ours. The two of them loved to sit together with me in the recliner and watch television. David was always a happy-go-lucky child." Following another brief moment of silent contemplation, Papa added, "For things to turn out the way that they did, well—" His voice trailed off. "I loved David so much."

Mr. Gyure was asked to describe an outstanding quality David possessed. After another thoughtful silence, he responded. "I don't know how to answer that other than to say he was always kind and polite to everybody. I've been trying to think for a longtime; about the boys growing up, and how things were, and well, they were my grandsons. David was my grandson. I never thought I'd have to label anything particular about him. To me, they were both normal, good boys. They suited each other."

After answering the first few questions, it seemed a little easier for Papa to open up. "I'll tell you a little story. David, Markie, and I went fishing one time. It wasn't too long before those two knotted their poles up and were having a heck of a time trying to get untangled. So I put my pole down to go help them. All of the sudden, they start to holler at me, 'Poppy! Your pole's goin'!' Well, a 23-inch bass was taking my pole." Mr. Gyure chuckled fondly. "That was it for them. They wanted to stop fishing and eat that bass right there." Mr. Gyure laughed. "And there was another time we'd went out night fishing. We were talking about different things and what all, whatever we were doing or talking about, David would be like, *'Thank you, Poppa. Thank you, Poppa'* all the time."

"After I had back surgery in 1992, David had somehow gotten out into the garage and ended up burning up my garage-door opener." Mr. Gyure laughed at the memory. "He was always so soft-spoken around me. I knew he could be rowdy but he was always respectful. I loved him to death, and still do." Papa paused and his voice lowered a notch. "I miss him."

It was difficult for Papa to talk glibly about his grandson but he continued answering the questions presented to him.

"Things important to David? For starters, I'd definitely say family. And then church and the Lord. You see, Big Mark always was a church-goer. So David (and Markie) went to parochial school." Papa stopped, "And his mom. David loved his dad too, but he sure did love his mom."

Mr. Gyure took an audible breath and continued in a rush. "You know, I think about this, how everything went around here. When people talked about David and what happened, you didn't hear the words they said but you saw the emotion. How about all the people he affected at his school so positively? I had no idea he was that way, that he was so well-liked, and loved. He was real serious when he needed to be but could clown around as required. He was a good morale-booster, for sure. When I'd call to talk to the kids or to Laurie (Mama B.), David was always the one who'd stay on the phone and talk the longest. Everybody else had things to do." Papa paused. "I'm sure other people have already spoken of this but you know, David had a bad feeling he wasn't coming back. Every time he'd call, he would voice concern about that."

"I'm so proud how students at his school recognized David; even still today. The amount of people who showed up at his funeral was, to me, mindboggling. I'd never been to a funeral like that. It was the most spectacular service I've ever seen in my life. Never once did I suspect there'd be so many people. It was amazing."

"Along the entire route were people who'd taken time to stand there as we went by. This wasn't even David's funeral procession at this point; it was when we were going to pick his body up from the airport. I never expected to see so many people saluting and standing with hands over their hearts. David's death touched so many people in so many different ways; normal, everyday people. I mean, there were fire trucks and so many huge flags; from Willoughby to East Lake all the way out along I-90 and back toward the school and church. It was absolutely incredible to see. I heard it was Northeastern Ohio's biggest funeral."

"There are so many things I've forgotten over the years, but every now and again, I'll see something and the memories will come back to me. I swear I hear something every day about David. You know, his name is on my truck. I get a lot of people coming up to me because of that. I guess I feel I have to keep his name out there. It makes me feel good how people can connect David to me. He's not just a statistic. David touched so many people. He was always so kind. When it came right down to the heart, he was a lamb; exceptionally kind."

"I had a young man, a Marine as it turned out come up to me in South Carolina and ask about David's name on the side of my truck. This kid had been out awhile, too. He told me he was in the 1/5 the same time David was. He and I talked probably two hours or more."

"We publicize the wrong things and forget about what we should be remembering. The people who contribute aren't getting the recognition they deserve." Poppy grew silent, thinking about what he was going to say next. "I remember the day I got the news. I'd been ready to leave out on my next run. Well, I'd left my cell phone in the house. I saw this car pull into the carport. It was my wife, crying. That's how I found out." He paused again. "I can't say how I felt. It was a hole that cut right through me. A part of me died that day. It was awful. I called work, told them what happened and," His voice trailed off. "I had nightmares about that day."

"I do miss him. I mean, nobody can know and I can't put it into words. David was my grandson. We shared a lot of laughs together. From the last time he called everybody like he did, that time he told me *'Papa, I don't have a good feeling with this.'* Even today, I can't express how much I miss him."

—WILLIAM WADE—

"I first met David when he joined the freshman baseball team at Riverside. He'd just transferred from Our Shepherd Lutheran School. It was his first year in public school. Besides being the coach, I was his chemistry teacher, too." Wade answered questions about his former student without reserve. "We acquainted well as player and coach. He'd help a lot at the bench and the other players got along well with him. David was a great team mate. My first impression of him was that he was quiet and reserved, an unusual young man. He had a sense of humor about him though. I knew his brother Mark a little better." Wade paused as he collected his thoughts. "When I found out about his death, well, in the first place, I never suspected David wanted to join the Marines. It all kind of caught me off guard."

"David Baker was a good kid. Always had a smile, was always helping others." Mr. Wade sort of snickered. "We always joked around. Have you ever seen the movie '*The Water Boy*? As a running joke, I called David 'Bobby', you know, after Bobby Boucher in the movie." Wade paused again as he thought about what next to say. "We'd always have a conversation when we saw each another. He was a genuine person all the way around."

"David wasn't a class clown but I think people were calmed by his presence. You knew what you were going to get with him. Every time our paths would cross, he'd be one of those kids who always said hello. David had good moral character.

He wasn't outrageous, just a genuine, wholesome person. I think any of his friends would tell you the exact same thing." Wade paused in thought. "So, in retrospect, I guess it really wasn't shocking that he went on to become a Marine. That's the type of presence he had."

"My memories are general. You have to remember, I'm a principal at a school with thousands of students. But David left a lasting impression on me. Like I said, every time our paths crossed, he'd always say hello. He had good moral character." Wade paused briefly. "His death was surreal. I think it was his sister Lauren who came in to tell me he'd been killed. It took me awhile to realize who his sisters were. I'm not sure which one it was now. But one of them came to the office to let us know. She sat down and told me and, I was in shock; that he even joined the Marines to begin with. I mean, you kind of profile kids, based on how they act in school. David seemed to me to be one to go on to college."

"I made the announcement about his death the next day. It was one of the toughest things I've ever had to do as an administrator. We honored him at a football game. And his funeral, well I missed most of the procession because I wanted to be in the church for his service. It was unbelievable. There were so many people, lots of support for the family—" Wade's voice trailed in fond reflection.

"The boys always kept in touch. It said a lot about who those two were as young men. They never forgot who meant anything to them." Wade's voice softened. "David's death meant something. I think that's what hurt the most. David wasn't going to be back."

"As far as what he'd be doing now, I imagine he'd be doing well at anything he set his mind on. I think he was still trying to figure out what he wanted to do and was going from there. He'd have been a great teacher. But whatever he would have done, he'd have been passionate about it." Wade drew a breath. "I guess that about sums up the type of young man I thought he was. His general presence touched people. I think he'll continue to make a lasting impact." After a moment of silence, Wade finished the interview. "When somebody dies, people say all kinds of good things about the person but David truly was that guy. He was the one who would always try to make the day brighter for everybody else."

—ROLAND MCNEIL—

"I had the honor of knowing David through different phases of his life. He was a really good friend to me." Mr. McNeil began after he introduced himself. "There are so many different elements that can be told about him."

"I saw him as a young man who had to make decisions in his life and was involved more as a mentor, particularly during his senior year." McNeil paused in thought. "But David knew where he was going. His life served a purpose, so important. He went into his military role wholeheartedly. When I asked him why he had chosen the Marines, he answered '*I'm so serious about this.*' It was the strangest thing, too because he was actually comforting me about his decision to go into the military."

"David was an inspiration. He taught me so much in life, even more in death. It's so unexplainable, almost surreal because he is still very much present. When he died, I was heartbroken. I can still remember the call. You hear about everybody else, the other people who died in service to this country but when I heard 'Lance Corporal Baker' it overwhelmed me. I mean, I know people are supposed to carry on with their lives, but it's been a difficult thing to do here, especially since he left so many emotions behind."

"I have to tell you this. When I met his nephew for the first time, Little David, I saw so much of his uncle David Raymond in his eyes. When I first picked that little boy up, he patted my back, as if to say, 'It's gonna be okay.' I didn't recognize the magnitude of David's presence in my life until he was gone."

"David loved his friends unconditionally. There was a conversation we had, where he actually said to me, '*Roland, I want you to understand something. No matter what anybody says, you are a great person.*' I was baffled by this. He was over there in Afghanistan and here he was telling me things to comfort me when it should have been me comforting him."

"The emotions I still have for my friend, I never thought they could run so deep. I can't say why things happen, but that call…" The sentiment was obvious in McNeil's voice. "You never think it's going to happen to anybody you know." He paused. "David's funeral was massive. It was as if time was standing still. People weren't grieving alone; it was rough."

"David grew from the end of his senior year to the time he went into the Marines. But this one conversation we had really affected me. The way he talked was unsettling. It was like he was saying his good-byes. 'David, you're talking like you're not coming back. Why are you talking like this?' and he said, '*I'll be back.*' I told him to be safe and do what he had to do to come home, to come back to us. But of course, he didn't come home."

"Those last moments were so important to me. David was comforting all of us while he was here. Imagine what he'd be doing now," said Mr. McNeil. "He was definitely wise beyond his years. His death was one of the hardest things I've ever went through. David will never be forgotten. There are so many different, important levels to this man who served our country. He was so proud, and gung ho, ready to serve, but by the end he seemed to know that he wasn't coming back. To me, that takes a certain type of individual, and it was the David Baker I always knew. I was so blessed to know this young man in my life. He was so positively influential. To this day, I still wear the dog tag bracelet bearing his name. "He had the ability and opportunity to perfect things. He was loved and still very much loved, honored, and appreciated. I don't think David's mission is done yet; not yet."

—THOMAS ISABELLA—

"I wasn't in the Marines with him but I was David's best friend before he left. We met when we all lived on Deerfield. I was six-years old when they moved in across the street. I went over to say hi and meet them and remember they had some Ninja throwing stars, throwing them around and stuff."

"We grew up around the neighborhood and hung out with the local kids. As we got a little older, I stopped hanging out with some of the bunch I used to; bad influences and all. David and I hung together throughout high school. I used to sit with him at lunch. After school, he'd come over to my house and play '*Call of Duty*' all day. He'd come to the school every day and we'd go see my girl. Our junior and senior years we hung out every, single day. That went by fast. Once we graduated, he joined the Marines and we were like, 'No man, why?' He enlisted right in the middle of all that shit going on over there. Infantry no less."

"Mr. Baker didn't like me when we were all younger. I mean, for one thing, I cussed; I never hid how I expressed myself. So David and I didn't get to hang out that much around his house. Like I said, we'd play '*Call of Duty*' and I'd go over to his house and eat all his dad's Cheese-Its. (Mr. Baker'd get pissed.) I'd go over and would always slide into their gravel driveway on my bike. It wasn't until I got a little older that people decided I wasn't so bad."

"It may sound strange, but David and I were so close that when we weren't hangin', I wanted to be. There were sometimes once in a while when he wasn't feeling good and didn't want to do stuff, but he was like a high point of my family. I remember one time when he went to Michigan to go see family and I had to go to Pennsylvania. I wanted him to go on our trip with us so bad. He was like my brother, but closer. I mean, I love my brothers but David was different."

"He was somebody you naturally liked; always happy and upbeat but at the same time, he was like a lost soul; my mom used to say that a lot. I guess Fate," Thomas paused. "—I felt like he was lost. You could look at him and know he was thinking about something else all the time. He was a great person. David would help out anybody he could without a second thought. I do remember a lot of those days."

Thomas was asked his opinion about what he thought the things most important to David were. Without hesitation, he responded. "His mom. His family. I mean, he absolutely loved his family. Money was never a deal with him, wouldn't have changed him. But if David'd ever won a lottery, he would have split it with everybody. That was the type of guy he was."

"When I found out he'd enlisted in the military, the Marines, I was like, 'Shit!' It was a bad time to enlist and what he had enlisted for—" Thomas let his voice trail off. "He fought for this country, which is awesome. He was a smart kid, was good-looking, and carried a good GPA. But he chose to go infantry."

"David looked like a shy guy, but he wasn't. He'd never act like a badass, but he was. None of us understood why he signed on. Even my dad asked him, 'You sure you want to do infantry?' and he was like, '*Yeah.*' We were all shocked because it was right in the midst of all that shit going on in Iran and Afghanistan. It wasn't a fun discussion, that's for sure."

Finding out. "It was one of the worst days in my life. I was pissed because I received word about it by text message. I was like, 'Holy Shit! No way!' I'd been studying for an exam that day, (which I did not take, by the way.) It was NOT a good day. It wasn't cold, but it was an awful, shitty day; it was gloomy. But you know," Thomas paused. "When autumn rolls around, it gets hard." After a few moments of silence, Thomas started his story again. "I went to his procession. My dad's a police officer and we had the privilege of leading. I also went to Arlington. (His was like going to a celebrity's funeral.) I had a friend in Virginia so I got to see him and went to the big military funeral. We ended up waking up late then having to drive like hell to D.C. We just missed David's funeral. But as we were standing there, it was only us three, like it was meant to be that way. I felt like it gave David's other friends the opportunity to mourn. It was good for his friends. I felt like that trip worked out the way it did for a reason."

"David was a big part of our lives. He and my girl Angel were super close. He'd always chauffer us around. David was with us all the time. Let me tell you a story. He and I went to this party. You've got to know, I didn't get along with a lot of people and every time we'd go to a party, I'd always get put out. But one night, David and Angel were out in the car. We'd gone to a party and it wasn't long before I was told to go. David was like, '*Fuck that! I want to go to this party. You always get kicked out.*' So Angel and I were out sitting in the car. She ended up puking all over the place. I decided to try to get her home while David was partying, so I took his stick shift and ended up putting it in the ditch. We ended up back at the house and had these two guys help us. I broke David's spoiler off the back so I kind of set it back in place. I told David Angel had gotten sick and he was pissed. So we leave the house and go to my grandmas'. All the way there, David was saying, '*This is bullshit. How could she puke in my car?*' We get to my grandma's and she comes out to ask what we were doing. I told her, 'Nothing' and David had me start cleaning shit up. He had to get something out of the trunk and when he opened it up, the spoiler went flying up into the air.

So the next day was like 110F out and his car smelled so bad. We were still cleaning this shit out and I was like, 'Can we listen to some music or something?' and he answered, '*This isn't play time, Thomas. This is 'clean David's car' time.*' So I asked him, 'Can we get some ice cream afterwards?' and he goes, '*Yeah, we'll get some ice cream.*' You'd take David seriously but he would say some funny shit. We had so many funny stories."

"We stole a keg one time; me, Mark, and David. We went to this party and there were about five kegs on the porch. I texted David, 'Let's try stealing one.' He said okay and I persuaded everyone to go inside. I dragged the keg to the edge of the porch to put it into my jeep. We got to his friend's house and said, 'We've got a surprise for you.' and we brought in this keg. We ended up taking it back the next day."

"One thing that may sound cliché was that David was genuinely a good person. He was, not like a prophet but he kind of was. I think he knew he was going to die. He'd have premonitions, feel things. You'll only meet a guy like him once in a lifetime. I have friends who are a little like David but nothing, nobody compares to him. The way he was, nobody compares…" Thomas's voice trailed off softly.

—MARK ANTHONY JACOBS—

"I first met David when we started working together. He was fifteen or sixteen. (I'm three years older.) David, his brother Mark, and I would all hang out quite often. I considered those two more like brothers, not just friends." Jacobs laughed as he shared, "Me and his brother were the first ones to get David drunk. We had some good times." Mr. Jacobs tone turned serious with his next remark. "David was one of those guys who was wise beyond his years."

"I guess sometimes when guys are getting ready to be deployed, some of them have this feeling, like they know whether or not they're going to be coming home. David pulled me aside and vocalized his premonition, saying, *"If I don't come home, get a tattoo."* I told him no way, to quit talking like that and asked him, "How about when you get back, we all go get some ink?' Well, I got mine; on my left forearm."

"Hard to think of only 'one best thing' about David; there are so many. He was one of the most trusting, sincere people; so straightforward. He'd give you his honest opinion, honest as a friend, rather than tell you something just to make you feel better. He'd tell you what you needed to know." Jacobs continued, "He had this great smile and always made me laugh. David had a great sense of humor."

"Family and friends were his first and foremost priorities. Then he joined the Corps. Being in the Marines meant everything to him. He slept, breathed, and ate Marine; everything for his country." Jacobs's voice lowered a notch.

"Initially, when David enlisted, I was kind of shocked. But I knew it was something he always wanted to do. I mean, he'd talked about it before, but when he went—I realized from that standpoint, to have somebody that close to me actually going, especially going to war and not knowing the outcome? It was kind of scary."

"David's death was the hardest event I've been through. I was at work and Mark had been trying to call me. He couldn't get through, so he sent Amy (my future wife) a message. She messaged me and I called Mark. He told me what happened. I had a hard time processing it. Then I saw it on the news. That's when it hit really home."

"I knew there were going to be people coming out to support the family, but was amazed to see the number that showed up that day. There were so many. All the people kept (that church) from getting anywhere near the family. It was a very intense day. It was a good eight mile stretch from the funeral home to the church and you couldn't have fit another person anywhere. There wasn't one empty space."

"Rover, the local radio personality from 'Rover's Morning Glory' had the song '*Chicken Fried*' on continuous loop that day. It's usually a classic rock station, but that day, he told everybody what was going on with that church from Kansas and he played that song over and over. Everybody tuned their radios to it, too."

"One of the best memories I have of David is right before he deployed for Iraq. I'd just started dating a girl a few months prior to us throwing his going away. That night, before he left the party, he pulled me aside. '*You're going to marry her.*' I told him he was full of it, but if it happened, he'd have to be my best man. Five years later, Amy and I married." Jacobs grew silent with thought. "I miss my best man, dearly. I think about him every day and would give anything to be able to tell him, 'Be careful over there. I love you man.' One more time."

"People who never got to meet David are missing out on a good person. For as young as he was, he was wise beyond his years. I think about him every day, reminding myself of the fact that there are still other people out there fighting for the same thing he was fighting for."

—ASHLEY OESTERLE, GIRLFRIEND—

"David and I first met in high school. He came to Riverside in the 9th grade from the Lutheran. He didn't know who I was but I happened to be standing in the hall with my best friend at her locker, who because of her last name, happened to be next to David's locker. We were standing there and I saw him.
"Who's that?" I asked her.
"David Baker. He's new."
"I vowed right there he'd be mine before we graduated. I knew he was the one."
"I was always attracted to David. Our relationship started shortly after I broke up with the boyfriend I had at the time. He and I had the typical high school relationship. My whole plan in my head was to eventually marry him; I mean, that might sound crazy, but I knew." At this point in the interview, Ashley's voice took on a soft, wistful tone. "When he actually told me he wanted to join the Marines, I was against it."
"Just before graduation, we broke up. He told me some of the most hurtful things and I was so heartbroken. So after graduation, he left and we much started doing our own things. After he enlisted and graduation happened, Mama B. and I happened to be talking one day. She told me David had done what he did because he didn't want me worrying about him while he was away. It was about a year after all that when I was out with some friends and happened to run into his sister

Taylor. She asked if I'd heard from David lately and I told her no. She gave me his number and I automatically shot him a text and well, we sort of picked up where we'd left off."

Asked to describe David, Ashley answered without hesitation. "He was a real smart-ass. He would torture me with jokes and, well," She paused in fond reverie. "—we always had a good time when we were together. He'd grab me and hold me in choke holds or we'd hang out." Ashley hesitated briefly before continuing. "He was the worst person for showing any real emotion. I always tried to bring that out in him. I guess he had a hard time showing his emotions to me. But he was an awesome person."

"David told me he was joining the Marines. Of course, I didn't want him to go. I automatically started thinking the worst. But I knew I was being selfish. I think of myself as being a very intuitive kind of person and I didn't want him to do it. But in the end, I knew I had to support his decision."

"The day David died," Ashley's voice wavered slightly as she continued. "—it was October and I was with friends picking out pumpkins. I mean, there were hundreds of people out there with their kids enjoying the day. It was supposed to be a fun-filled day and we'd planned on doing hayrides and picking our pumpkins and everything. Well, for some reason, I'd left my phone in the car. When I got out to the car, I saw I had about 20 missed calls and 50 text messages from people I hadn't heard from in ages. So I immediately called my friend Nikki to find out what was going on. 'Did you hear about David? You need to call his mom.' She asked me where I was and told me I needed to sit down. I told her to just tell me what was wrong."

"'David died today.' That was it. I screamed and fell to the ground. People were stopping, kids were looking at me, nobody had any idea what was going on. I was in shock. It was such a nightmare."

As interview processes continued, Fitzgerald was given to find out about a letter in David's belongings he had written yet never mailed to Ashley. His best friend in the Marines had the task of going through his belongings and had found it. Asking Ashley about the phone call she received regarding that letter, this is what she said.

"Getting that call from Steven was strange for me. The whole letter thing happened the following summer, 2010. I wasn't doing very well at the time, still grieving over David. Mama B. had texted or called me (I can't remember which) to tell me I was going to be receiving a call from David's friend in the Marines. 'He has to tell you something, he has something really important.' A few minutes later, I got the call and Steven told me he'd found a letter that David wrote about a month before he died but had never mailed. (It was long, too; almost four pages.) News of that letter came at the most perfect time for me. I needed something. It was almost like David wanted me to receive that letter as a message."

"It was nice knowing he'd been feeling the same things I was while we were broke up but at the same time, it was so sad. We were supposed to be together. My life is not what it was supposed to be, and I've tried so hard. Nothing is ever going to be the same." Ashley grew silent as she gathered her thoughts. "But I know I have to try."

"I wanted to share a story about the time I surprised David at the airport. I've already briefly mentioned the time we started dating again, when I'd texted him at Applebee's. Keep in mind the fact I hadn't seen him since high school graduation because he was stationed in California and had been deployed. Well, David was coming home for a couple of weeks, so Mama

B. and I had the awesome idea to surprise him. Of course, I was so excited. I'd told David I wasn't going to be able to come up to Painesville when he was home because of school and work obligations but that was a lie."

"So I'd left Columbus, making my way north to Cleveland. I probably was going ninety-five miles an hour because I was so excited. I drove straight to Mama B.'s nonstop. I was early for David's flight so we hung out until it was time to leave for the airport. I was nervous and excited; feeling so many emotions all at the same time."

"When we arrived, we found ourselves in a bit of a pickle because only family was allowed past the gates, which was understandable I suppose but there was no doubt in our minds; I WAS GETTING THROUGH THOSE GATES! Mama B. and I ended up going to security and begging them to let all of us through. We told the security guy I was David's fiancé and I was surprising him. Mama B even gave me the wedding band she was wearing to put on. We were prepared to do anything at that point because our boy was coming home! The great thing about it all is we got through!"

"We practically ran to the gate but had to stand around for about 20 minutes. Mama B. was finally like, 'I see his plane!' We found a hiding spot for me behind this huge pillar in front of his gate. People started unloading, it seemed like a million people were on that plane and of course, David was one of the last ones to get off. I remember seeing his reflection in the window walking up. He had a big smile on his face as he walked towards his mama. Then I came out of hiding. The look on his face was priceless. He looked like a 5-year-old on Christmas morning seeing all the presents Santa had brought. The feeling of jumping into his arms was amazing. I literally leaped at him like a panther, clutching my arms around his neck and never wanting to let go. I couldn't stop giving him kisses. On our way home from the airport we both sat in the backseat holding hands, staring into each other's eyes. I wish I could feel that again."

"I hide my feelings but it's a hard thing for me to get a grasp on that I have to go the rest of my life without him. It's not fair. I can feel him sometimes, I dream about him. I feel like that's how he communicates with me." Feeling the interview drawing to a close, Ashley had one more thing to say about David. "He was such a loving person. I want people to understand what he sacrificed. He loved this country, his country and ultimately lost his life because of that."

The Last Letter David Wrote to Ashley as Shared by Ashley Oesterle

Ashley,   8/2/09
How's everything goin? I'm doin ok. I've been doing a lot of thinking on this deployment about my future. This is it for me; no more military come summer of 2010. I don't want to live my life in regret. So I've been thinking about where I want my life to go, I hope at this point of your reading, you can see where I'm going with this. I don't know if your dating or in a relationship, but that doesn't even matter because I want you to know how I feel anyway. You know I hate to write and to show my emotion but I don't want to regret not doing something or to pass something great up. So I'm putting my heart on the line for you to either stomp all over or for you to do something about it. You might laugh at this or you could believe that I truly mean every word I write down and it comes from my heart. All right, so here it goes.

All right, after the last deployment, we broke up when I got back to the states. So I decided to let loose, party, do whatever I wanted. I did this thing about not caring about standards, so I slept around for a little bit. Then I came home for x-mas, we hung out for two days. I had fun at the bar with you and also enjoyed talking to you at my mother's house. That night at the party, I was only trying to get on your nerves when I said, "Who's easy?" to the other girls. Also I didn't hear or remember you saying for me to come see you before you left for Columbus the next morning.

After I left to go back to Cali (California), I began to think. I said, "Why look for better when I had the best?" It's taken awhile for me to write this. I tried to call or text but I don't think you wanted to talk to me or something. I meant what I said when I said I still love you and you said it too, maybe because I said it or maybe because you meant it. I guess I will find out when you read this. I'm still in love with you and I want you back in my life. I know I have changed since you saw me last. I think you are the one and I pray to God you have those same feelings for me. And also after I left home, I stopped sleeping around cause it wasn't getting me anywhere in life. I can't stop thinking about you. I love you with all my heart. I know when we were together you said you would wait for me til I got out. I know times have changed and so do feelings for people, but I hope you still mean that. I will have the up most respect for you. I can't change my sense of humor but I can tone it down. Either way if this doesn't happen I still want you to know I will do anything for you. I hope I also can tell you in person. One reason I write this now at this time is because I don't know what could happen to me out here.

I know I can make you happy. We have history together so I hope that this isn't moving too fast for you. I know a lot about you and you know a lot about me. If I could have it my way, this is how I would go by doing it. I would come back home, we take things very slow, no physical stuff because I don't want that to complicate things. I would love you with all my heart Ashley. I'm not asking you to marry me, but what I am asking you is to give this another chance. I want to see you happy and if that's not with me then I'm going to have to deal with that. I know we're good together. I would like to be the man in your life. I miss you. Yes, this is a love letter.

I think about what career I'm going to study in college, but I can't get past not having you in my life. I want to always be around you. Something came to mind. Remember when we were dating when I was in the USMC, I seemed excited to see and talk to you but when I got home it wasn't like that. The reason wasn't that I wasn't excited; I was overwhelmed for one being home to see my family, friends, etcetera and the military thing. I had a lot of things on my plate. Too many things to do when I go home for leave and things that people expect me to do. I was stressed out.

I love you, I will always love you, whatever you need I'll be there for you. I may be an asshole at times and I don't care, but I think I changed. You have never heard or seen me do something like this. I'm not doing this to pass the time because I don't have time, I'm doing this because I want you in my life and I want you to know how I feel. I'm nervous you don't feel the same way. I'm actually more nervous you moved on, than me being in Afghanistan. I'm not desperate in general but I am desperate for you.

I want you to know I love you, we can make this work and I see it going well.

With all my love,
David

P.S. Just kidding. No, but for real; I mean every word! Ashley Marie Oesterle I love you, I can't help it. Don't freak out I know this is random and out of left field.

—MATTHEW KOHLS; DAVID'S UNCLE—

Speaking with the vast quantity of Marines, friends and family members about David Baker revealed the remarkable spirit that was and still is this Marine. The loss of the extraordinary presence Baker lent to so many people's lives continued to be a difficult path for many to tread. Yielding to the author's request for detailed interviews regarding David's biographical account was often an emotional event but it was those particular interviews that spoke volumes about the young Marine named Baker.

When speaking with David's uncle, Mr. Matthew Kohls in California, it was immediately apparent by the fondness with which he spoke that David's presence was still close in his heart. Discussing qualities his nephew possessed, Mr. Kohls revealed the following.

"One of the things at the foremost in my mind, to say what captured the essence of David is the fact he always had a tender soul. He was a loving and thoughtful young man, but tender is the best word to describe him. David never took anything for granted. As I said, he had a kind soul and that kindness wasn't limited to just people, either. He showed the same consideration for animals as well. I recognized that quality in him. It may not be something anybody would expect to hear about a Marine, but that was David."

The next question presented to his uncle Matt concerned sharing thoughts about David as a child. After deep contemplation, he answered the question thoughtfully. "David always liked to laugh. When he was happy, he always expressed it in such a way that touched my heart. People might not know this, but David had a sweet voice. He would sing and wouldn't care about who was listening. He loved to sing. A lot of the songs he would sing were his Sunday School songs—" pausing briefly, Matthew added "it didn't have to be Sunday to hear him sing, either."

"As a little boy, David would occupy himself without a care as to what the rest of the world was doing. He could always bring joy to the moment. I thought that was a great quality for a young child to have. He would be the kid content with a blank sheet of paper and a crayon. David had a great imagination, too. It was a natural gift. I absolutely loved that about him. He was always a pleasure to have around. You know, our educational system tries to bring that trait out in children, but David? He had it naturally."

"David had an unconditional love for people. It didn't matter the circumstances. It didn't matter what kind of situation was at hand. I think that helped him through the times that growing up weren't as easy as people liked to think it should have been for David and his brother Mark. He was nonjudgmental. It made me very proud. I loved him so much and that particular quality in him meant so much to me as the years went by." It was obvious Mr. Kohls was putting much thought into his next words. After a brief pause, he spoke again. "I don't know any other way to say this other than David always loved me for who I was. Both my nephews, David and his brother Mark were amazing examples of pure love and acceptance in times that proved difficult for others in my family. They loved me no matter what the circumstances were."

"I remember one visit in particular with David. He and a bunch of his brother Marines were in California and they all came to visit. We had a great time out on the beach in San Francisco picking up sharks teeth, playing music. It was a bunch of young men hanging out together on the coastline who were so missing their families, getting ready to go on deployment. I felt that visit was so beautiful." Matthew stopped abruptly before continuing in a melancholy tone. "That was the last time I saw David and I will never forget that as long as I live; the day was perfect. I have such good memories."

"You may have been told about the family cottage we have in northern Michigan. Well, David loved the annual trips we took there and had cultivated some wonderful, lifelong friendships. And even though our family essentially migrated to Ohio, everything at the cottage up north stayed the same. The friends he had there and kept in touch with, they've kept in touch even after everything happened. We went to the cottage and his friends would still come over and share stories about times with David. There's no words to describe it other than that David was held in such high regard by most all the acquaintances he made in his life. People always wanted to be around him. He had great charisma. David absolutely loved going to Sand Lake. As a matter of fact, people up there showed up in Ohio to pay their respects at his funeral. They were all there and it was phenomenal."

"When I first heard David had joined the Marines, I was honestly like, 'Oh my God!' Why?' We offered to assist with paying for college thinking that was what was making him so inclined to join. That was my first reaction. We wanted him to go to school, but he was interested in becoming an MP. David had always wanted to be an MP. At the same time, I respected his decision, but I felt like I had to give him an out. I had the ability to help him out but he truly desired to join the military. He had a serious conversation with me where he explained how he'd have opportunity to take advantage of his GI Bill once he got back. I did have opportunity to see him before he was shipped to Afghanistan. He was so proud to have followed through with his desire to join. Before he shipped, he said, *'I'm going to make the best of this. This is the path I've chosen. When I get out, I'm going to earn my degree.'*

"David was almost done with his military obligation when he was killed. When his dad (Matthew's brother AKA 'Big Mark') called to tell me what happened, I was like 'I feel like I just saw him. This can't be happening.' I wanted to be with my family immediately so I flew out to Ohio as soon as I could to help where I could. It was all like a bad dream."

"David was the kind of guy who would always step up to the plate, like it was for him to walk point. If a job had to be done, he'd take it head on."

"One thing I was proud of David for? It's something his Marine brothers Steven and Trever told me. Over in Afghanistan, there were always little Afghani children around David, all the time. He loved children and always carried candy in his pockets for them. I was like, 'Why are there children always around him in these photos?' and they stated, "David always had candy for them. It was something he liked to have them look forward to."

"Something else about David; he dedicated some time toward humanitarian efforts and children over there inclusive of women's education. He was instrumental in providing a safe-haven for children and girls so they would have a place to go and get an education. This is something I would always say, if it wasn't for us going over there, women would still be getting shot in the head, wearing burkas, and experiencing oppression all of the time. This was something David helped to combat. He wasn't there for war. He was helping them in their community. He made the very best of a bad, horrible, situation. I'm sure he gave women and children hope; inspired them in many ways."

"I've come to learn over the last few years of his life, that David put his faith out there unconditionally. I believed he shared his devoutness with his colleagues and they respected his authenticity. David never made any bones about saying how Jesus had his back. What you saw was what you got with him. He had no ulterior motives. When you bring your whole self to a job, being authentic is a wonderful quality. He was still trying to find his way in life, but he was definitely authentic. He had no hidden agenda."

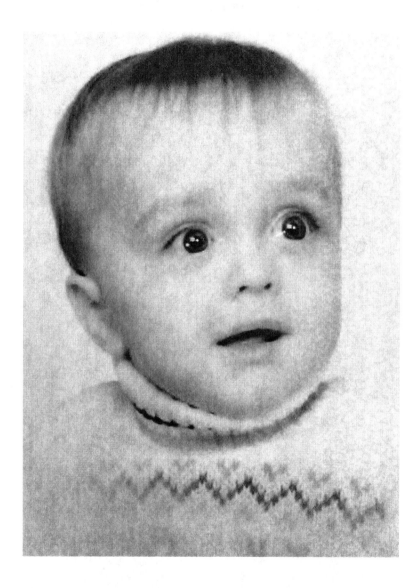

PART II

"THIS IS THEIR STORY"

"There are those among you although young, who have already suffered a full measure of grief and sorrow."

Dieter Uchtdorf

SUCH GOOD MEN

(Adaptation of Michael Norman's "These Good Men")

Note: Author Fitzgerald read this adaptation at an annual Veteran's Memorial Service held in Mentor, Ohio the same weekend in October when the first interviews with Baker's family took place; David's birthday weekend.

"I now know why men who have been to war yearn to reunite. Not to tell stories or look at old pictures, not to laugh or even weep. Comrades gather because they long to be with the men who once acted their best, with men who suffered and sacrificed, men who were stripped raw, all the way down to their humanity. You did not pick these men. They were delivered by fate and the U.S. Marine Corps. But you know them in a way you know no other men. You have never given anyone such trust. You were each willing to guard something more precious than each other's life. You each would have carried one another's reputation, the memory of each man lost. It was part of the bargain you all made, the reason you were so willing to die for one another.

You cannot know where you are headed. Yours are not perfect friendships; those are the province of legend and myth. A few comrades drift far from you now, sending back only the occasional word. Know that one day; even these will fall to silence. Some of you will stay close, and a couple? Perhaps always at hand. As long as you have memory, you will think of them all, every day. And each of you can be sure that when you leave this world, your last thoughts will be of your family and your comrades in arms…such good men."

> *"No day was typical. You didn't want typical because typical meant routine and routine could mean the difference between life and death."*
>
> Cpt. Clinton Hall, USMC

Each interview comprising this section underwent several edits. Verbal consents were obtained before interviewing began and owners of said interviews had express right to edit, omit, rewrite and/or add to in any way, shape, or form, up to the last opportunity before the final edit. Any interviews that were given yet not included here is likely result of an accountability factor.

In each case, what began as multiple interview processes each turned into a single medium ultimately painting the portrait of one amazing life.

> *"Patterns reveal how the world works."* In his book, 'The Mission, The Men, and Me: Lessons from a Former Delta Force Commander', Pete Blaber speaks of recognizing them. *"The most effective weapon in any battlefield whether it be combat, business, or life—is our minds ability to recognize life's underlying patterns."*

"How do we end up doing what we do in life? How do we become what we become? How did we get where we are today? At some point in our lives, we ask ourselves these questions. Of course, there's no single, causal explanation or answer, but by looking back through the pattern revealing lens of hindsight, we can recognize some of the defining activities, experiences, ideas, and opportunities that ultimately shaped our paths."

—SSGT. NICKOMAR SANTANA, USMC—

"It wasn't until nearing the final edits of this biographical account that the author asked me for the favor of contributing a little something extra. I have to admit, it was a difficult decision considering how much responsibility was involved. Generally speaking, whenever somebody writes anything about a Marine, there's more than simply crossing T's and dotting i's to contend with. I questioned why anybody would want my input about somebody I did not personally know. I considered myself a mere pebble in the pond full of much larger boulders. But in searching for the answer, it became clear to me. I may never have known him, but by Baker's death, I lost a brother. *Every* Marine lost a brother. In putting pen to paper and creating an introductory piece, I looked at it as a chance to begin this Marine's story a second time. In accepting such a monumental task, I considered my thoughts carefully, making sure what I was about to share would not only be reflective but also significant."

"It's for that fact that any Marine who has died in service to this country continues to live on in everyone who wears the Eagle, Globe, and Anchor. It's our responsibility to remember them all. A too often overlooked fact by the rest of the world is how for us, the loss of a brother isn't a cross for just friends and family to bear. His brother Marines remind mothers and fathers who have lost children to our lifestyle that although they may have lost one child, they have gained thousands more. It's all a part of being a Marine. It's what we do."

"Marines aren't so much made as they are born. Those yellow footprints aren't there for decoration. They are a testament to the scores of individuals who have committed to a balance of three things to earn the title 'Marine'; honor, courage, and commitment. Many men have tried, and yes, some have even died trying to claim the title of Marine."

"With honor comes a sense of duty. Then determination. There has to be a feeling of resolve, compulsion, and obligation to make a Marine desire to not just 'be' a Marine, but to be an exemplary Marine. A Marine must have the courage to fulfill his duty as charged and be committed to see things through."

"Marines often find themselves at the receiving end of criticism and condemnation from the public at large. We do what we are told to do, being duty-bound to obey direct orders. That's not to say Marines never question those orders. It's a Marine's duty to question the validity of every order handed to him. The decision to follow those orders fall on that Marine's moral compass, a compass tempered by society long before that individual ever turns into a Marine. Duty-bound doesn't mean unquestioned."

"Being a Marine entails more than just presence. It means sacrifice and servitude. That may seem archaic, but it's accurate. It's similar to religion, except for a Marine, servitude isn't only to God but to the people and the Constitution as well. I know as a Marine, I've chosen to sacrifice my own freedoms so the people I serve can have theirs. Not everybody wants to stand on the front line and face the enemy. Not everybody can, but somebody has to. Sacrifice is not only the ability, but also the choice to deal with the things nobody else wants to.

Marines see that and however way they understand it, they answer the call.

"Some join, intending to serve their term of enlistment and get out. Some join with all intention of serving for life. Some enlist and get their chance to serve but don't get the opportunity to come back home. None of them serve with any less conviction than the other. They have all earned the title of United States Marine."

"At some point in their life, each Marine has a defining moment. Whether it's while answering the call to serve their country in the first place or during some unexpected moment they fell upon in country; they answer to something beyond a regular man's comprehension. Ronald Reagan summed it up best with this quote; "Most people go their whole lives wondering if they made a difference. Marines don't have that problem." Nobody may ever know what defining moment transpired for Baker, but rest assured, it happened."

"So as far as a beginning? There was a need. And now? There's still a need. How have Marines specifically contributed to that? They've fought for freedoms, for rights of others who could not fight for themselves and they've fought for the Constitution of the United States. Marines have been in it since the beginning in 1775, and they're still in it today. Whether it's from the halls of Montezuma, the shores of Tripoli, Korea, Afghanistan or Iraq, Marines will continue to do what they do and protect those who need to be protected. Becoming a Marine specifically to accomplish that? Some will make it and some will not. It's that simple. Baker was one who made it and today, he's not alone in the ranks awaiting the Lord's review. This Marine is still serving, serving instead from where only the angels tread."

(As posted by Mark Baker Monday, 04 July 2011 at 0440, "A poem a friend of my brother's wrote for him after his death." Used with permission from William Warren Childs, USMC.)

—BROTHER—

By: William Warren Childs, USMC

Here we are today
With bottles in our hands.
To honor you, fallen brother
In a far off distant land.
Rest now my brother
And wonder not anymore.
For every breath you shall not breathe
We shall breathe one more.
We honor not your memory
But the life you never had.
No wife to call you sweetheart,
No child to call you Dad.
So gather round all ye friends
And hold your bottles high,
Here's to you fallen brother
We toast you our good-bye.
Rest now my brother
And wonder not anymore,
For every beat your heart shall not
Ours will beat one more.

———

—TREVER SIMPSON, USMC—

"I first met David on ship on the MEU (Marine Expeditionary Unit). He was in first section and I was in second. Before we went on our first deployment, we got glommed in together with a bunch of other Marines. So how we met up and became friends was by Fate I guess. It wasn't until after we got back from deployment that we started hanging out. It was me, him, Steve, and John—always together in Steve's little hatchback Ford Focus. You could find all of us together every weekend."

"One of the first things we did together?" Simpson sat contemplating, deep in thought before responding. "SOI; School of Infantry. He hated it as soon as we got there." Trever laughed heartily. "Sure, I guess there was a sourness to it but after we were in for a little while, we settled in and started thinking, 'It's only for four years.' We were all making plans for what we were going to do and where we were going to go to college after everything was all said and done, you know, planning on life after life in the Marines."

"I think it was at Twenty-nine Palms and we were getting briefed by this colonel who'd just gotten back from Afghanistan, I mean just got back like only hours before. He was talking about how *'Perfectionists always fail because they're too focused on getting perfect at something instead of just taking what they have.'* So, we started screwing around with David, joking around about his wanting to be a perfectionist and that he wasn't going to make it far. We were just messing with his head, is all."

***Are there any particular stories you recall and would like
to share about David?***

"Oh yes. There was this 'ole cat named Jimmy Beran. Good
'ole Jimmy." Trever paused and laughed out loud. "Jimmy
and David were roommates up to our first deployment. Beran
was one of those good guys, you know, the kind of guy who'd
never give in to peer pressure or do anything bad. Well, they
were having a 'Field Day' (think cleaning your living quarters
from top to bottom, eight hours straight) and you know, no
matter how much time you actually spent cleaning them, the
showers always fail; no matter what. And Jimmy, well, he had
a broken leg. So instead of cleaning the shower, David had
Jimmy stay in the shower so they wouldn't go in to inspect.
Beran was on limited duty at the time because of his leg so he
didn't have to do what everyone else was doing."

"The guys were waiting for them to come inspect quarters.
Jimmy was sitting in the shower with the water running for
like three hours, just waiting. David made him stay in there,
too. Beran wanted to get out and David got all serious and
was like, '*No! You stay in there.*' He made him stay in there
the entire time." Simpson guffawed heartily as he shared the
story.

"One time, we'd been out at Denny's and had a little
situation happen where the cops ended up coming out and
questioning everybody. Nothing came of that so we decided
to go back to the house. It was around 0200 and we were all
drunk so we decided to go to San Diego to see these chicks
John knew. By the time we get there, David has passed out.
Instead of waking him up or anything, we just left him in the
car and went on inside."

"The girls were drinking wine out of these fancy glasses and had candles lit all over the place. Steve and I looked at each other and were like, 'Screw this' and grabbed a few bottles of wine and just started drinking straight out of the bottles. We were being real asses. Anyway, Steve goes to use the bathroom to take care of business and in the process clogs the commode. So what does he do? He decides to use one of the girls' toothbrushes to unclog it. He cleaned it off, comes out and says, 'We've got to go.' This whole time, David was still out in the car. While all this has been going on inside, David woke up and was like, '*Where am I?*' He didn't know where he was so what does he do? He pulled out his phone and called his friend Thomas up in Cleveland, Ohio. He told Thomas, '*Hey, look up this intersection for me.*' I guess Thomas asked him, 'Where you at?' and there's David, '*I don't know. Somewhere in southern California.*' So Thomas looked up where he was, and found him in southern California. By that time, we all were coming back out to the car. David was pissed."

"That's usually what most of our weekends were like, or they'd end up turning into something like that. The four of us were tight. The way we connected with one another was like, everyone would gang up on the guy who'd say the dumbest thing, like if I said something stupid, everybody else would get on to me about it and start harassing me. The only way I could stop it would be if I could come up with something to turn things around. We'd go like that back and forth with each other all the time."

David was a man of faith. Was this something obvious to those around him?

"Definitely. Actually, let me tell you a little story about that." Simpson paused and looked around the dining room before continuing. "It was a different night, but of course we'd all been out drinking in San Clemente and decided to go for some McDonalds. Matt and I were having this discussion about God and here's David, right? No matter what Matt or I would say, David would just fire back at us with all these facts and religious stuff he'd learned, telling us how ignorant we were for saying the things we were saying. All of a sudden, David decided to call his dad back east. It was like 0300 in the morning there but he woke his dad up and started talking to him about God and religion, telling him how Matt and I were being idiots and retarded and, well it just showed how he wouldn't back down. It was his faith. That's how hard he believed. He definitely stood his ground and thought nothing of proving you wrong. I mean, we were all drunk that time when he started going off; but that was the only time he'd get like that."

"He was upset on the phone. Matt and I were sitting there thinking how we hadn't meant to take things that far. David was frustrated with us. I mean, he was so pissed and was like, '*Fuck you guys*' but I think he knew we didn't think the way we'd been talking. We were doing it just to get under his skin. At the end of it all, he was like, '*You guys are assholes.*' I'd definitely say, without a doubt David truly believed. It wasn't for show, either."

David's Brother Mark, also sitting at the table, also commented on Simpson's responses: "We'd both went to private school; Parochial school at the Lutheran Church. Our schooling made his faith that much stronger. I couldn't ramble off all the books of the Bible to you now, but you know, we both could before. We had to memorize Bible passages and stuff every week."

Mama B.: "I remember in church, David would sing. He was just a little boy, about two years old or so and when the whole congregation would sing, David would sing out with 'la-la-la' or 'aahh' or something. And he was loud. When everybody else was done singing, David would still be doing his baby-singing. Everyone would turn real quiet after they'd finished and there was David still singing away. The pastor wouldn't speak; nobody would start another song until David stopped. Then, the pastor would begin the next song or start his sermon."

It's been said David knew he wasn't coming back from Afghanistan. What are your thoughts about that?

Simpson: "David knew."

Mark: "He said he knew; more than once. And the last phone call he made? I knew that was it. I knew it, too." Mark paused a few moments before continuing. "I was actually at the airport waiting for Maxxine at the gate and David was calling me for phone numbers. He just kept calling. He'd call, ask for a number, get it and hang up. Little while later, he'd call for another. He did that over and over."

Mark's voice was more solemn as he continued. "You know, I've had a few friends who said the same thing about not coming back; and they didn't either. I think people already know; like they get some sort of hunch, accept it and forgot about it. I had one friend who didn't go out on patrol one time and his entire bunch got ambushed. He said he'd had a bad feeling and told the rest they shouldn't go. Three of them ended up not coming back. Every time David and I happened to talk about it, he didn't stress about it. He was like, '*If it happens, it happens. I know where I'm going.*'"

Mama B., who'd been sitting nearby, listening to Simpson and Mark quietly, added, "He never seemed like he was afraid—" She trailed off.

Mark: "I'm sure he was; but for everybody back here; not for himself."

Mama B.: "Well, like when he wanted to plan his funeral from out-of-the-blue. He said, 'Mom?' and that's when we had the pickle jar conversation."

Mark: "He wouldn't veer away from the subject, either. I mean, he knew it was going to happen, plain and simple."

Mama B.: "There was one time he told me, '*Mom. They told us we're going to come back missing something. Arms, legs, hands,*' and he said, '*-Mom, you know how I like to wear flip-flops.*'"

Mark: "I think he was worried about being a burden to anybody else. I know I wouldn't want to have anybody help me up the stairs or get me dressed."

Mama B.: "I told him not to worry. We'd get ramps built, and do whatever we had to do to accommodate him. He was so worried about wearing his flip-flops. Just like Mark said, it'd come up in conversation, (death) but he was never sad about it."

Where were you when the events of that day in October happened?

Trever: "The day everything happened—" Simpson drew a slow, deliberate breath before continuing. "David's patrol was sort of southwest of my position. I was at PB (patrol base) Flemming (which was about three to five miles from

David's base.) They'd been out patrolling, and had already found some bombs. We'd heard about the controlled dets (controlled detonation of unexploded IEDs) and a couple of IEDs. I guess they were coming up on these compounds, sweeping for bombs. David had his wand (metal detector) out and was getting ready to test it when he stepped out and—" Simpson swallowed hard before responding in a noticeably softer voice. "I guess that's when he stepped on a pressure plate. It came over the radio but at that moment, they didn't name names. I didn't find out specifically until later that night, because of the mission they were on. They were out in the west pushing down, so all we'd heard over the BFT, (blue-force tracker: computer and GPS based system that provides individual soldiers and commanders with location information of friendly military forces) was that there was one Marine KIA, two wounded, and nobody knew who was what. I want to say I think I was the first person at our base to find out because I happened to be in charge."

"Even though he died somewhere around noon or thirteen hundred I didn't find out over the BFT until around nine or ten that night" Clasping his hands behind his head, Simpson let out a deep sigh. "Oh man. Like I said, I found out over the radio. My first response was disbelief. I don't know." Simpson's voice trailed off again into silence. "First they listed what had been accomplished on the mission that day then there were details about what happened. From that list, they read off 'The angel watching over us tonight is LCpl. Baker.' At first, I couldn't believe it. So I reported back, 'Are you serious?' I mean, I just couldn't believe it. The staff sergeant responded, 'I wouldn't joke about something like this.' It was my responsibility to inform the other guys on my shift."

—MATT GERMAN, USMC—

"The news gets everything wrong. The world needs to know."

"As far as how Baker and I first met, well…it was Fate. I mean, obviously we met through the Corps but we'd started out at different boot camps. We just happened to be assigned to the same unit after SOI. We were near the same time frame as far as enlistment went. At the time, he had less than a year to go before he was to be discharged."

"Baker." Matt German spoke David Baker's name with a fondness apparent even over the phone. "David had a gift. I mean, oh my God, he was funny. I remember when we were coming into our first unit and you know, we were at the bottom of the totem pole. Most people were all serious and, well, David was the relief. I'd say, hands down, he was the funniest person I've ever met. He was a clown when he needed to be, so funny. No matter what the situation, no matter how desperate, tired, or hungry we were, he'd lift everybody up."

"David was a personable kind of guy who could relate to and would talk to anyone. He never had any problems with anybody. Sure he was a joker, but in a Marine sort of way. That's hard to describe. See, ideally people don't get upset. You learn one another. You're not just Marines, you're brothers. You can't get mad at things and still be effective to get your job done. But morale is important. David knew this, but he also had the ability to realize the seriousness of a situation."

Matt paused before softly adding, "More than all that, Baker was a friend. That's what he was, a damn good friend."

"And as I'm sure a few other people will tell you, Baker was also a Grammar Nazi. If you spoke and were grammatically incorrect, he'd correct you for sure. Like, if you said, 'Me and him are going to the beach' David would automatically say, '*He and I.*' You'd be like, 'What the hell?' and David would repeat himself. '*You're supposed to say 'He and I' are going to the beach.*' I think that's why he liked hanging with us so much. We drove him absolutely insane."

"David was funny." German paused. "It's hard to describe him; but not really. I mean, he was who he was. You either liked that or you didn't. But let me tell you, I never met a person who didn't like David. He was one of those guys people automatically felt comfortable going to talk to. You asked about attributes, well," Matt paused in thought "—I think there are a few different aspects to that question. Like physical attributes? David had these great, big, blue eyes you noticed even before he opened his mouth." It was obvious German was putting a lot of thought into answering this question. He paused at some length before finishing his answer. "Mentor. David had leadership qualities. He let people know he could be a leader. You see, I was his squad-leader and had the responsibility of taking care of my group. But when things would get rough, he'd just know." German paused. "Like I said, he was a great friend."

"David was an all-round good guy to have around. He took on other people's troubles and tried to make light of things. While we were in combat, he was more worried about other people's focus. During replica training exercises, the only emotion he wore (so to speak) was to keep everybody positive and happy all the time. I mean, people were just so happy to be around him. He never experienced or showed fear, outwardly. And sadness? No. Happy, filled with joy. I know at one point he had some girlfriend issues back home, but even then he would make jokes. He'd just push everything aside and be like he was; a happy, go-lucky dude."

"Patrol Base Brannon. In a day's work, we'd do approximately 16-hours of patrolling; have four hours of fire watch in some capacity and maybe three to four hours of sleep. You also had to fit time to eat, do laundry, and do whatever in there somewhere. Sometimes it was different, like at times you'd be out for longer than 24-hours, or sometimes you'd do night patrols. Typically you'd have around 15 Marines and maybe 20 Afghan soldiers together. There were always thoughts in the back of your head about 'What if?' with those guys. David was almost shot by one, actually. They were just jacking around and one of the Afghans pulled the trigger on a machine gun. Obviously, it missed David, but not by much. You have to be ready for anything. I mean, there were thoughts I guess, but nothing ever happened. Afghani's have the heart but not the training. About 15-minutes before David died, one of the Afghans got hurt bad. That was a hectic hour time-frame for sure."

"Patrol the day David died," Matt took a slow, deep breath before continuing the interview. "Our patrols were usually six to eight Marines with the same number of Afghan soldiers. That particular day was part of a giant patrol spread out over a great distance. We were on a two-day mission to clear the area of IED's, bad guys and whatever else was in the way. We were scheduled to leave 19 October and head back 20 October. So all total, there were probably 40-50 Marines in all but we weren't all on top of each other. It took a long time for everybody to get to us after the explosion happened."

"It was my decision to do what we did on patrol and as a result, David lost his life. As the leader, I was responsible. There were many negative effects but at the same time, the whole situation made me reevaluate my own life. 'What's the point?' You know, the majority of people over there (in Afghanistan) didn't know. It was like, 'Why am I doing this?' Then I look at what David's life was," Matt paused, deep in thought. "I heard a quote by this man named G. K. Chesterton; *'The true soldier fights not because he hates what is in front of him, but because of what is behind him.'*"

"*'Marines don't fight because of what we hate; we fight because of what we love, because of what we left behind'.* David embodied that. I know I can't take the weight of the whole country on my shoulders, but I can take the weight off my friends and family. In and of itself, it was definitely tragic somebody so young died fighting for this country. David definitely knew the risks. I mean, we trained for it, we prepared for it," German's tone grew hushed. "—but David chose not to focus on that fear (which, by the way, if he had any fear, he never showed it.) I'm saying the world is a lesser place without David Baker. I gained a whole new perspective on life because of him."

"If anyone asked about what was important to David, I'd have to say family, of course. And his faith. But the first was family. I mean, this was extremely evident in how he respected his mom, his dad. There wasn't any doubt he loved them. If he were still alive, I could see him as the ultimate American family man." German chuckled with recollection. "Ultimate. He would definitely be the one who'd take every opportunity to crack jokes at other people's expense but he wouldn't do it if he thought they couldn't handle it. He absolutely loved his brother and sisters," Matt paused. "There was no doubt but he wouldn't hesitate to poke fun at them, either."

"I was a single guy, didn't have a lot to live for. We were a bunch of single, young men who thought we had nothing to lose. After David was killed, I valued life more, particularly since David lost his. I gathered my perspectives and put them in better order."

"I have a story about David. We were in the states at the time, out in southern California, which is notorious for beautiful weather and beautiful women. For some reason not apparent to me, I had some music on my iPod that David liked particularly. So, we got in my truck, and I think Simpson and Aragon were with us and we went to Laguna Beach to hang out and cruise around. We also went surfing and what not, as well."

"About those songs; David loved them. He called them the 'Girl-Getters' because if you're a guy and can sing, girls really dig that. So David would roll the truck windows down and sing these songs to the world, not caring what anybody thought." German laughed heartily. "On a more serious note, let me tell you. It showed you who David was. He and I did a lot of planning together. We were peers. We had a great friendship but an outstanding work relationship. He and I would sit down and make plans on how to ultimately achieve our goals in defeating the enemy while we were in Afghanistan."

"There was one specific area where we'd always get into in a fire fight. Always. It was in or around the same area where he ended up being killed. Anyway, there were a lot of mixed demographics in this area. We had a well-educated informant here, a doctor from Afghanistan who bluntly told us that he worked for both sides. So David and I would come up with all these plans for patrol maneuvers. We'd make plans then we'd split into squads."

"Off they went. There was a road going south and one village right there and then another village farther on up the road. That area was where all of our enemy contact took place. Between the two villages was a hillside we used to draw enemy fire and stuff to complete our mission. We started down this ravine that blocked us from sight. Unfortunately, the enemy knew this too and had placed a claymore in the path. Now, David was point man. He'd already gone through the tree-line at the pomegranate orchard. I mean, you could see through it. Well, I was 20-30 feet behind him when he suddenly yells for me to stop. I see him grabbing this string and just kind of holding it there. Come to find out, that string was attached to the claymore which was aimed right at my head. The string was a trap. They (the enemy) are watching so they know when to pull it. They had actually started pulling the string and David caught it, just in time to keep it from being set off."

"David was always a good guy, a number one guy for sure. You know, he ALWAYS volunteered to take point; he sure enough did. He never thought of himself, always thought of others. When I was squad-leader and had to appoint men to positions, I never had to worry about point. David always volunteered."

"Afghanistan is not like they show it on the news. I mean it's a desert but, it's not like what they show, what they want you to think it is. Where we were at the time things happened with David, there was this one area of vegetation, but where this all occurred was 300-400 meters from our patrol base (Brannon). We were just heading south down the road, pretty much guaranteed we were going to see some action."

"Taliban are smart. People forget, we trained these guys. They're a bunch of 40-50 year old men who use their heads. We were on THEIR turf, and they know that, too. Like, take for example the fact they will usually only attack at dusk or dawn. You have to adapt to that type of thinking. It's not always easy, but we're Marines and that's what we do."

"Afghanis are little, short people. But this one guy we'd see was like 6'4; big. He was high in society, too. But the majority of them are short. As for myself, I never saw an Afghani female. Afghanis are constantly watching. They see you long before you see them. We could overcome the terrain but we never had to fighting an enemy who doesn't wear a standard uniform. This has probably been the most difficult war America has fought. It was hard to distinguish who we were fighting at times. For all intent and purpose, your enemy is the entire civilian population. But there's ways around that. That's what establishing good rapport is all about. They'll tell you who the shitheads are among them and what they've done."

"The day everything took place, we had some Afghan soldiers get hurt. (They had stepped on an IED that was set up just inside a doorway.) We were in the Valley and David came up and asked me what I wanted to do. I told him to take the rest of the team up on the hill and that I'd finish with the Afghans and that situation there. So they pushed out away from our position below and maintained security for me and the birds (helicopters) that came in to pick the guys up. So Cameron, Santorro and Baker were all headed to the cemetery across the way. We were going to meet up on the backside of the building. David was told to pull his metal detector out and he was all like, '*O-kay*'. I firmly believe David knew what was going to happen before it did. He put enough distance between himself and the others (which he never did) so they weren't right on top of him. I was watching; David kept walking while he was running his tests on the detector. I told him to quit walking and run his God-damned test. He made eye-contact, looked at me and actually winked then seconds later, he was gone. One of those things you hear stories about all the time, but I saw what I saw. David *knew*."

"When it happened, I was like, 'HOLY SHIT!' I went into Marine mode and ran up the hill. I ran through the debris, all the rocks flying from everywhere. I had to get to my guys. I didn't want to confirm it was David, but I knew. I was yelling for another Doc to get over there, 'Come help these guys!' When Doc Clemons got there, I was able to evaluate the situation. Everybody heard me on the radio and they'd heard about the evac from Cameron and Santorro. When someone dies, you don't say their name over the radio. You just say, 'There's one KIA.'"

"It's so emotional but you have a mission to complete. Ultimately, you have to keep going. I was pissed when I got told that, but we had to complete the mission. Meanwhile, back at base, they'd put it all together; they knew our KIA had to be Yenowine or Baker. They didn't want to accept it either way. They watched us come in, and when they didn't see David, they knew."

"I think Simpson was running his own patrol base and I might have sent message to let him know what happened. I'm not sure what I did that day. You know, when your patrol returns to base, that's supposed to be the time you unwind, rest. You don't want to jump right back into things. If you're all emotional and whatnot, it's not a good time to debrief. I think we ended up doing all that the next day. Then, like I said," German stopped abruptly, regaining his composure.

"We all loved David, but we had a job to do and we were gonna fucking do it; especially after they took our guy. Everybody seemed so incredibly focused. We completed the mission; no holds barred."

"The grieving process began after we all came home. You see, morale is a big thing in combat. Your men have to be ready and willing at all times. Your men's' ability to focus is a direct reflection on you. You have to just unload and forget, be ready for anything. After the IED went off and David was killed, people wanted to bomb the region, 'No. Leave it up. We already know the area. If we do anything, they'll just do something somewhere else. We already knew historically that was where they went to do their thing. We needed to use that information to our advantage.'"

"Roll Call at COP (combat outpost) Sullivan; we called Sullivan '*The Mansion*' (An unfinished residential compound seized from a local drug lord). I took part in that. I carried the rifle, did the drill movements. I was ecstatic to be able to have participated in it because you know, not everybody could even go to this ceremony. It was a hard time, too because of course everybody was grieving over the loss of David's life but I put my grief aside and honored the man. There's not a day that goes by I don't think about him, not a day I don't pray thanks to God I'm still alive. I was thankful I got to pay my respect and honor my friend."

"David's death affects my life today, absolutely. Let me explain this. I was right there when everything happened. To me, at the time, it seemed my life was over as well. Not in the physical sense but like, 'How am I going to go back home and tell people I lost a guy in my squad?' David was physically gone; wouldn't be going home to eat, drink, talk like the rest of us. During down time, I'd get to thinking about it; survivor's guilt I guess. It's gotten better but I still think about it." Matt took a moment of silence. "As a direct result of David Baker and what happened, I'm currently working on a college degree to go back into the Marines as an officer."

"Until just recently, I was thinking about it all the time; the nightmares, I mean, I SAW it happen." German's voice rose slightly with emotion as he continued his interview. "I visited Arlington last summer and was almost overwhelmed. Over there, (in Afghanistan) we didn't have time to mourn. When he stepped on that mine, we couldn't skip a beat. We had a mission to complete, to focus on or else none of us would have made it back. When we finally got stateside, I had another mission. I was worried everything would come flying back; but strangely enough, I was at peace. I held the decision I made against myself; until I visited Arlington. I felt at peace, sitting there talking to David just like old times. We sat there, hanging out and it felt so good. Healing has moved me forward. Not that I'm ever going to forget David, but he wouldn't want people mourning and moping over his death. He'd want us to have a beer, have a good time, because that's who he was. I firmly believe he doesn't hold anything against anyone. A lot of us are still alive today because of David Baker."

"You never forget. I'll never forget Baker or anybody else I might lose in the future. These guys knew what they were doing, the potential sacrifice they might have to make the very day they signed up. Marine Corp infantry? You're probably going to war. We were aware that fact was there. 'What am I fighting for? Do you believe in it? Yes? No? Unsure?' Then don't do it. Things happen. It's a scary thing. But would you fight for your family and ultimately what you stand for? David said yes. I said yes. We all said yes. There have been a lot of great men in history who've said yes. I can't think of who said it, but there's another quote that goes something like this: '*If you don't die for something, then you've lived for nothing*' David never had that issue. He knew what he wanted to do. "You have to take a stand."

—THE FRENCH FOURRAGÈRE—

Not unlike the United States Government and Military, the French government has awarded special decorations to its military forces (ribbons, badges, etc.) for achievements and accomplishments as well as for especially meritorious conduct. Decades ago, during 'The Great War', (better known as World War I) the French awarded over one hundred and fifty military units two particular such decorations; the Fourragère and the Croix de Guerre.

"The Croix de Guerre is given as either an individual or unit award. It's a medal awarded to those who have distinguish themselves by acts of heroism involving combat with enemy forces. "When a unit is mentioned twice, it's awarded the fourragère of the Croix de Guerre. This fourragère is worn by all men in the unit, but can be worn on a personal basis: those permanently assigned to a unit, at the time of the mentions, were entitled to wear the fourragère for the remainder of service in the military. In the United States military, the Croix de Guerre was commonly accepted as a foreign decoration. In the modern age, however, it remains one of the most difficult foreign awards to verify entitlement. This is since the Croix de Guerre was often presented with original orders, only, and rarely entered into a permanent service record. [20]*

Today, members of United States 5th or 6th Marine Regiments and the Army's 1st BN 28th infantry regiment,* *are authorized to wear the fourragère on their left shoulder signifying that brigade's award of three Croix de Guerre during the First World War, but only while that individual is assigned to the unit. Wearing of the decoration is considered ceremonial and the fourragère is not entered as an official military award in permanent service records."* [22]

—MICHAEL HATTON, USMC—

"They told me I was the reason David joined the Corps."

"I knew David from school. I actually graduated with his brother Mark in 2004, but I knew who David was." Mike answered. "I can't remember for sure, but as far as his first impression on me was probably, 'Who is this cocky little shit?' But he was a good kid; always made everyone laugh." Since Mike had schooled with David's brother, I took opportunity to ask about David and Mark's relationship. "They had a good, brotherly relationship. They razzed one another for sure but they were always there for each other when they needed to be."

"David was dependable, always the good guy who did the right thing. He was one of those people who whenever he was around, would always set you at ease; could always make you feel relaxed." Mike took an extra moment before continuing with his question. "David was outgoing. But he was also honorable. Trustworthy. Dependable. I honestly don't think there's any better way to describe him than as an honest, wholehearted, good person. There was never anything negative to say about him. David was just a good person."

"I'd gone back to Riverside High School to speak about being a Marine. I was walking down the hall in uniform and David come up to me and randomly pulled on my fourragère. (David was laid to rest wearing the same fourragère he'd tugged on at the school. There's a story to that.) I told him he shouldn't pull on the stuff on anybody's uniforms and I let him get away with it since I knew him. He started talking about joining the Marines. So he signed up and ended up getting assigned to one of the units still authorized to wear the fourragère."

"After David died, we went to the Cleveland Hopkins airport to receive him from Dover. Cheno (David's recruiter) was escorting him and had to do inspection at every stop. David was all squared away when he come in from Dover except he was missing his Fourragère. I happened to have mine. So when he came into Cleveland, that's when he got my fourragère."

Mama B. filled in more details to the French Fourragère story. It didn't stop at Arlington; that time.

"Some time after the service at Arlington, one of my dogs (Tootsie) started carrying on at the house, frettin' and wanting to get into my room. So I opened the door and the dog dove in, going directly under my bed. That's where I'd stored David's garment bag. Tootsie was just beside herself trying to get at that bag. So I finally pulled it out and opened it. Tootsie crawled in and immediately laid on one of David's shirts. I got to looking around in there and found David's fourragère. I knew exactly what to do with it."

"After David died, Mike Hatton's wife threw Mike a birthday party. I decided to give him David's fourragère as a gift." Laurie paused briefly. "I didn't know how he'd react so I decided to go give it to him before the party, as an early present. I put it in a little bag and away I went."

"I had no idea what it was at first." Mike remembered. "Laurie had stopped by to drop off a gift. So when I took it out, that's when it hit me; like a ton of bricks. It's hard to describe how it felt. I was so honored she even wanted to give it to me."

Laurie said, "He opened it and started to cry. The fourragère had come full circle."

I asked Hatton what he thought were things most important to David. "Family." He said without hesitation. "Family was real important to him; and the Corps, and doing the right thing. As far as him wearing any of his emotions on his sleeve, from what I'd seen being around him, you had to know him to be able to see or know when anything was wrong."

"I was already out of the Corps when David deployed. I was out landscaping the day I found out he'd been killed. My little brother called and asked if I'd heard about David. I was like, 'No. What happened?' He told me everything he knew. I dropped what I was doing and called Mark, who confirmed everything my brother had told me. I went home, grabbed my wife and we went straight to Laurie's. I was actually hesitant to go at first," Mike stopped "—because she'd told me I was the main reason David had joined the Marines."

"When we arrived at the house, Laurie gave me the biggest hug in the world. It lasted so long. I guess that's when my feelings changed. I knew she wanted me there and I was actually relieved. I mean, I didn't know how she was going to react. From that moment up until we all went to Arlington, I don't think there was a single day I wasn't at the house." Mike paused as he searched for his next words.

"David's wasn't the first military funeral I'd been to since getting home." There was an audible change in his voice when he spoke again. "I went to Arlington with them. Like I said, his wasn't the first military funeral (I've actually been to more than I'd like to remember) but it was my first one in Arlington."

"I wasn't there when this happened, but I've heard the story a million times. David was home on leave and he and his brother had gone out drinking. David had this thing about all the time yelling, 'FIRST!' Well, fast-forward to Arlington. Cheno had family who lived near Arlington and they had arranged for a service at their church the night before the big service at Arlington. Well, long story short, during some segment of that service, we all decided to yell out 'FIRST!'"

"I spoke at the church service and read a beautiful poem I'd found. I've not read it since that day but I pulled it out and decided to share it." (That poem is included in this book.)

"David's death definitely still affects me. I had a great deal of guilt for a while, blaming myself for him going in and going infantry like I'd done. I had a hard time going to their house for a while, too until they changed things around. (Mama B. had essentially dedicated her living room as a shrine to David's memory.) I mean, I had to pack up 95% of my own Marine stuff." Hatton paused. "Based on my experiences in life, a person never gets over losing somebody the way we lost David. But you have to learn to live with it. There's always going to be bad days." Hatton's voice trailed off. "I'm not putting *any* of the guys behind me but I'm still learning to cope with everything."

"When David completed his enlistment, he'd intended to buy a Chevrolet Camaro; flat black (They didn't make Camaros in flat-black.) but he was killed before he came home." Mike paused as he recalled the story. "Laurie still went out and bought a Camaro. And you know why she named the car Hootie, right?" Hatton asked. "'Hootie' was David's nickname."

"David's brother Mark was getting married in California. So when Laurie flew out there, I went to the house and basically stole the car. I took it and had 'Hootie' custom-etched over the doors and took it back to the house, put it in the garage and covered it back up."

Mama B. added to the story. "Mike (Hatton) and Mark Jacobs picked me up from the airport. It happened to be David's birthday, so Taylor'd been at home making a cake and David's favorite meal, something she does every year. So we got back to the house and Mike told me we had to go out and look at the Camaro."

"I couldn't keep it a secret. I didn't want her to be alone when she discovered it so we told her we had a surprise."

"The cover was on the Camaro and Mike started slowly pulling it back. I didn't know what the hell they were doing. I thought one of the kids had taken it out and messed it up or something and that's what they were going to show me."

"Laurie wasn't sure what she was supposed to be looking for so she followed our eyes and saw what had been done to the car. She started to cry immediately and gave me one of the biggest hugs ever." Mike finished telling his part of the story.

"He'd had 'Hootie' etched over the doors, real subtle-like. It wasn't real bright or bold or glaring out at you in any color. It looked like ghost writing." Laurie added to the story. "David had wanted a real bad-ass car when he came home. When Mike did that, David's car was complete."

—THE LEGACY CONTINUES—

(Memorial Day Weekend, 2013; Arlington, Va.)

"In my Father's house are many mansions: if [it were] not [so], I would have told you. I go to prepare a place for you."

John 14:2

There was an almost spontaneous decision for David's family and many friends to converge upon Washington, DC and Arlington for the official start of summer in 2013. However, just a few weeks prior to that, Fitzgerald had received an invitation to attend a School of Infantry (SOI) graduation ceremony in Jacksonville, North Carolina at Camp Geiger. The invite had been extended by Staff Sergeant Nickomar Santana who was graduating his first class of Marines.

During the course of that weekend, Fitzgerald was given opportunity to tour Camps Geiger and Lejeune and discuss locations LCpl. Baker (and thousands of other Marines) had himself been present at when he began his enlistment as a United States Marine. Before the visit that weekend was complete, Staff Sergeant Santana had determined he and his family would be present for the weekend in DC, "But don't rat me out to Mama B. I want it to be a surprise."

In the months leading up to May 2013, many people were planning how to access Washington and Arlington, Virginia to pay their respects to all of the fallen. That weekend was a bittersweet one for Baker's family for the fact that it not only saw them all convening at Arlington section 60, plot 8856 but it also marked the anniversary date of David's unit being deployed to Afghanistan in 2009.

May 2013 was invariably cooler than the previous year and found those who gathered at Arlington wearing hoodies or hastily found jackets ordinarily left stashed in the backseats or trunks of cars. The morning came for everybody to converge upon the Nation's capital. The ultimate destination, of course was Arlington National Cemetery and with it being the Memorial Day Weekend, hundreds of people were expected to do likewise in paying respects to their own. It was decided everybody would meet at the gates at 0800 that Saturday morning with Mama B. obtaining visitors passes for everyone to drive to Section 60. She and the rest of her immediate family had left Ohio around midnight the night before and headed straight for Arlington. Fitzgerald had arrived in town the evening before and was one of the first people at the gates that morning; the first one for visiting with Baker's family. So she called Mark to find out where everybody was at in the scheme of things and as he answered the phone, she couldn't resist: "FIRST!" She could almost hear the smile in Baker's voice as he very matter-of-factly responded, "Oh, so you're going to take that, are you?" Fitzgerald acceded to Mama B. "Nope. Your mom can have it. She gets FIRST."

Fitzgerald placed her next call to the family Santana to pinpoint their approximate time of arrival. Things were moving along just as planned.

Everyone was standing by at the gates at Arlington as Mama B. and the rest of her entourage arrived. She immediately dashed into the visitor's center to secure passes for everybody's vehicles. While she was inside, Staff Sergeant Santana and his family arrived, taking their place in line with everyone else. Santana was in full dress blues, ready to surprise Mama B. Fitzgerald was standing on look out to alert everybody when Mama B. came out of the visitor's center. As the Santanas were taking information from David's brother Mark about getting to section 60, Fitzgerald sighted Mama B.

"Go! Go! Go!" She rushed the Santanas ahead as she sited Mama B. Mama B. had heard Fitzgerald and thought the author was hurrying her on with the "Go! Go! Go!" command. The Santanas successfully eluded Mama B. but just barely.

So committed was this mother that when she made it through the gates, her immediate instinct was to beeline straight to David's headstone. Mama B. completely bypassed everybody already assembled there, including the Santanas. After a few moments, Mark drew her attention to the fact the Staff Sergeant and his family were there. Operation Dress Blues was a tremendous success. This was only the beginning.

The morning was chilly but bright, with the sun shining high in a beautiful blue sky. Throngs of people were at Arlington besides the party with Mama B. with a number of folks gathered in the vicinity of Section 60, plot 8856 tending to their own missions that morning. Some stood in contemplative silence and personal reflection while others simply observed the moment as it unfolded. Staff Sergeant Santana had been given to hear the special story regarding David, Mike Hatton and the French Fourragère that was part of the uniform of Marines who served with the 1/5. That morning at Arlington, Santana decided to add to that tale.

As readers may recall, prior to David enlisting in the Marines, another Marine named Michael Hatton had visited David's high school to talk about the Corps. In the process of the day, David had approached Hatton and in an instant akin to tugging on Superman's cape, David tugged on Hatton's fourragère, asking him, "*What's this all about?*" Long story short, David enlisted and ended up assigned to one of the units still authorized to wear the device. When the incident in Afghanistan took his life and he was brought home, it was discovered by his escort John Chenoweth and Michael Hatton that his fourragère was absent from his uniform. Michael gave David his own device and that's the one David was laid to rest with. Mama B. later found David's fourragère in one of David's garment bags and presented it to Hatton for his birthday. With the course of events following as such, Staff Sergeant Santana determined to give Mama B. his own device since she no longer had one in her possession. Closure. That morning at Arlington, Staff Sergeant Santana respectfully presented his own fourragère to Mama B.

It was a bittersweet morning of reserved contemplation for all in attendance. Even the younger children present behaved exceptionally well. It was as if their little hearts understood the magnitude and brevity of the day, the place, the moment. They each in their own way paid respects not only to David, but to others at rest as well. The love and respect shown by all who gathered in Arlington that weekend was conspicuously displayed. With her family, her Corpsmen and Marines, Mama B. only reluctantly walked away from her flower upon a star.

—STEVE ARAGON, USMC—

"I first met Baker when I entered the fleet at Camp Pendleton (California). As soon as you finish MOS (military occupational specialty/job) school, you go to Fleet. (You're still called a 'Boot' there and that's where the weeding out process begins). We were picked up by this Master Sergeant from Weapons Company and were the first Boots to enter the unit. My bunch had already been together a few days and we knew Marines from East coast were coming. We were all waiting to see what they were going to be like. That was the first time I met David. We didn't talk in the beginning. I mean at the time, it was like an East vs. West Coast thing. But as soon as they got there, we were all in the same platoon. We didn't hang out for a few months. David actually disliked the Corps at the time. I liked it just fine. While I probably took my job too seriously at first, he wasn't like that at all. If truth be told, we didn't get along; not at first."

"My first impression of Baker was that he was a nerdy, skinny, East Coast, white boy. He was the type of guy who did what he had to do without ever complaining, however, he always had something to critique. David liked doing what he had to do, was proud of doing what he had to do but didn't like the politics. He always had something smart to say."

After a long, thoughtful pause, Aragon continued. "David was an all-round, stand-up kind of guy. He stood out, had his opinions about things. One time we were having this conversation about religion. He'd always stand up for God.

When it came right down to the nuts and bolts of things, David always stood his ground. He was fearless; never scared or anything. He wasn't like 'tough-guy', "I'm going to kick your ass" kind of fearless or into picking fights or anything but," Aragon paused "—he'd be the guy who'd always have your back."

"I was in a different section at the time now that I think about it. Something had happened between me and Simpson and somehow, our staff sergeant had caught the air between us. So he'd put me into a different section. Anyway, when one of our guys had been shot, David stepped up. He just wanted to get things done, and you know, not everybody was like that. When our guy got shot, there was this other Marine who didn't want to go out anymore. David stepped up and just did what had to be done." Aragon paused. "I know he felt like he wasn't coming back, definitely. I'll always believe he had a premonition he wasn't coming home."

"Baker was the guy who could always make a person feel better. He was that guy who could hang out with anybody because that's who he was. If you were having a bad day, he'd feel for you then try cheering you up. It was through another Marine I even came to know him in the first place. David and I hadn't talked very much or hung out. This other Marine and I were more friends first because we'd done boot camp together.

One day, something was happening between David's girlfriend and an old boyfriend of hers so David and I started this conversation about what was going on. It was after that when we discovered we actually had a lot in common. So, that's kind of how things went. In the beginning, we didn't talk at all but after that first deployment we started hanging out together. One by one, our little group came together and then we were all together every weekend."

"David was never the type who'd complain to anyone about his own problems or anything. He stood up for the underdog. He was the guy anybody could go talk to about anything. David was blunt when it came to that. But most of all, I'd have to say David was a family guy. I mean, he was always was talking about his mother and father; all the time. His family definitely came first; they meant everything to him. I mean, I'm sure you've seen pictures. David actually had the word FAMILY tattooed in huge letters across his abs and this enormous Celtic cross on his back and Jesus on his shoulder. So you could tell, literally just by looking at him; his 'Family' always was before him and God always had his back."

"Patrol Base Brannon. What did we do over there? In a word? Patrol. We'd either get into a fire fight, or not. We'd walk around a village, talk to the people, and try to build rapport with them. There'd be times we'd have fire fights, and run across IED's or there'd be times we'd come across nothing at all. It was literally hit or miss."

"We'd patrolled this one southern town (the same town where David was later killed) and had come in the back way, through these pomegranate orchards. While we were patrolling, David happens to see this kite string and starts pulling on it. What he actually did was pull a string away from this guy (an Afghani) who had intended to detonate an IED. The guy had wired it wrong or something. The IED wouldn't have gone off, but nobody knew that at the time. So we stopped what we were doing and had to wait hours for EOD (explosive ordinance disposal) to come and do their thing. In the meantime, we started talking. Once we'd detonated the actual IED and looked at everything that was in there, we were all like, 'Damn.' We'd actually had an IED incident before that one but we were the only people in our platoon that had hit an IED."

"There was a sniper platoon attached to us and they'd been compromised. So when that happened, there wasn't anybody else on base. There were only twelve of us there to begin with, but those other guys needed to be picked up so in order to do that, the rest of us went out to get them, taking a route we usually didn't take. This explosion happened and I got thrown back into the truck. There was so much dust. We had checked outside for any possible secondary IED's but nothing happened. So there we sat, waiting to get picked up."

"The night before, the company was making its final push through the Nawa district. David and I were on watch together in the tower. David had reached a point to where he just couldn't stand being in Afghanistan any longer. *"If I could just go back in time to start a new life, I would do it. Just forget everybody."* I asked him if he wouldn't miss all his friends. At first, I thought it was a sort of selfish thing to say, but after he died I realized the pain he left behind for everyone and think I finally understood. If we never knew him, it would have saved us the tremendous hurt we felt when he died. The last thing I said to him before he left on the mission was 'Don't get blown up.' We had a sick sense of humor between us."

"When David was killed, I was angry, of course. I felt so helpless. I mean there we were, doing our thing and my friend gets blown up before my eyes and I couldn't do anything about it. The war didn't stop and that was the worst part, getting over it or at least not thinking about it because we still had the job to do." Baker wasn't the only loss this Marine had experienced. On 10 November, little over a month following the explosion that claimed Baker's life, Aragon endured another friend/Marine's death. "After everything happened, there weren't many people at our base and our sergeant wanted some of us to stay behind. He made me stay at Brannon while my squad went out. I was upset about having to stay at base." The morning David Baker was killed, there'd been two Afghanis wounded as well.

"David's patrol was headed back to us at the base and a helicopter had been called in to get the Afghanis out. This other Marine and I were up on com in the watchtower talking back and forth when the explosion happened. Over the radio, they said 'One casualty, one KIA' and at that moment, I kind of already had this gut feeling it was David. There were a lot of activity going on, and everybody knew we had a KIA, but you know, names don't get broadcast It took them about fifteen minutes before they got back." Aragon's voice dropped. "One of the guys looked at me and shook his head. That's when I knew for sure."

Aragon continued, taking frequent, audible drags from his cigarette. "I was okay by the time Roll Call happened. I mean, I couldn't cry anymore. I guess it hadn't hit me at that point what happened. When the explosion went off, I was like, 'Fuck.' I knew David died. I just wanted to see my other friends." After some moment's pause, this Marine continued. "I don't know. Yes, it still affects my life. I think about David every day, especially when times are tough. I guess we've preserved the pristine image of him, the way he was. I see how the rest of us are, and the things we're all experiencing since getting back but, that's not what's in my head when I think about Baker. Time just stopped."

"As far as being deployed over there; if things would have been different, who knows? It wasn't long before everybody started questioning all the shit we were doing. For instance; we had no electricity, or running water, right? Doing our jobs, making do with what we were given and then having the higher-ups wanting to get onto us about not having haircuts? David couldn't stand that shit. He was tired of it. Brass would come around and be like, 'Some of your Marines need haircuts.' I mean, we were bathing out of water bottles, no running water at all, taking 'showers' like that maybe every couple of weeks and their big bitch was about our haircuts?"

I asked Aragon if he had any particular stories from Afghanistan that stuck out about David Baker. "One time, David and I made this solar powered shower. At the time we did this, there were this bunch of social scientists out there as well who had us taking them around town and stuff. One of them was a retired colonel. Well, I was in our set up taking a shower and needed David to help me get something off my back. So he was in this shower with me and that colonel overhears us. 'I don't know if I should be listening to you guys.' And I said something back like, 'You know how it is Colonel. Sometimes you need somebody to wash your back.' There are so many stories. Like I said, David always had your back."

"We went to a party at this apartment in San Clemente, California. We were Infantry Marines and when we went out, we just wanted to have a good time. So, we went to this party and there was this girl who David and I both tried to hook up with at the same time. Well, it wasn't working for either of us so we just gave up and decided to go to Denny's instead."

"That's how David was. One time, we decided to take a trip to Vegas. When nine 'o clock hit, we were completely obliterated. I mean, a whole group of us were out having a good time. David was so funny, one of the funniest guys I've ever known. There's so much to tell about him. Like, I had this girlfriend who absolutely adored David. We decided to go to this club in Arizona. We were trying to get David to hook up with this overweight girl and he was like, '*Fine, I'll do it.*' Well, no matter what he did, that girl wouldn't have anything to do with him. So then he was like, '*I can't believe she turned me down.*' David also accidentally ratted me out about another time in Vegas that my girlfriend didn't know about."

"There was this one day in Afghanistan; we were in the area south of the town where David was later killed. A dog came running after me from out of nowhere. I told this guy to put his dog up, shot a warning shot and it ricocheted. Well thank God I did that because inside the house were these Afghanis waiting there to ambush us. David walked right out there and started shooting back, bullets whizzing past us and everything. I was like 'What the hell are you doing? It's not worth getting shot just because you're not scared.'"

"The week leading up to David's death, he and I had been out on every single patrol together. That week, we were actually getting ready to get out of there. We had one big push south of where Hall (Captain) was, a little south of where we were."

"As for being in Afghanistan, there were too many times we were undermanned, ill-supported but, (pause) we had to make things work. The biggest thing I've taken from this is the fact David would have wanted people to really think about what they get themselves into before committing to anything. He was a certain kind of person because of all the different things he'd experienced up to that point. Then he got to Afghanistan and was like, '*Wow. Why couldn't I have just thought things through?*' But I guess everything happens for a reason."

—SCOTT SANTORO, USMC—

"I first met David probably within a week of arriving in California. I can't remember the exact date. I wish I could, but I just can't remember everything. I can tell you this though, he was hilarious. David always found a way to make people smile. He's hard to explain. I mean, he could do things in ways without actually meaning to pull people together, but he did it. It was the weirdest thing." Santoro fondly recalled.

"David could say something to somebody that was bad but you'd laugh and get over it. Other people, you'd be pissed off with—but with David, you'd understand that was just who he was and you'd get over it real quick."

"What many people don't understand is David and I were inseparable for about two years. We didn't go anywhere without each other. So besides being as funny and outgoing as he was, David was also a personable and faithful guy. His family meant everything to him; family and faith. But friendships ranked right up there as well."

"We were on a two-day mission, coming back to base. We were getting close and knew we were going to be hitting home soon. We hit the first IED and it got two ANA soldiers. Me, David, and Staff Sergeant Cameron were injured. It was nerve-wracking. This was the first one I was involved in. The next IED…we were walking toward a graveyard." Santoro's voice grew soft. "It was hard to have any emotions at the time. I had shrapnel in my eyes and it was hard for me to see." Searching for the next words, Santoro continued cautiously.

"I didn't have emotions about my best friend dying because I wasn't sure. I'd been badly injured myself at this point so there wasn't much emotion for me until later on. It didn't sink in because of my own condition at the time."

"I could tell you everything about that day; the way it smelled, the sites; everything. I mean, I knew I wasn't going to die but it was hard to think about anything else in the world when there was something so terrifying going on right in front of us. I think it took a while for people to realize what was going on." Santoro stopped speaking for a brief moment as he again collected his thoughts. "People see each other leaving camp all of the time so it didn't seem like David was gone, like passed away, gone."

"Roll Call at Pendleton was probably one of the saddest moments of my life. That was another time it hit me. David wasn't the only guy we'd lost but he was the only one I knew." Santoro was almost done talking. "David's death affected everything. He's sometimes the one who keeps me going. If there was just one thing, well, I can't pinpoint just one thing. He was a good friend, a good person all the way around. To name just one thing about him would not be giving everything else justice."

"I do things today I don't even realize. He had such an effect on me. I'm sure he did everybody."

—DANIEL 'DOC' CLEMONS, USN—

"Somewhere in my third year (I guess it was January of 2009) I was attached to David's unit; First Marine Division, the 1/5 ('one-five'). It was an immediate gain, too. The first formation I went to, I introduced myself and David said something that immediately made me laugh. I instantly thought he had to be some kind of real good person. It was there I first met David Baker as well as Matt German and a few other guys."

"Growin' up how I did, I hung out in some real ghetto neighborhoods. For most of my life, I was around very negative people. So my first impression of David was completely and totally opposite. I mean, I'd been around lots of different people and could just tell that David was a good dude. If the world had a light to it, that would've been him. He had a big heart and he genuinely cared about people. You could just tell he was a great, great, man."

"I remember one evening during some kind of training we were having, David and another guy were getting into it." Doc's thoughts shifted direction. "But you know, despite whatever differences they may have had, in the end well, let me just tell you. That other guy? He ended up getting a memorial tattoo in honor of David. When all was said and done, even that guy's life was affected by David."

When asked about significant qualities Baker possessed, Doc Clemons responded proudly; "How can I pick? I'll give you my favorite two. For the first, well you have to know

David wasn't a judgmental kind of guy. I mean, he'd call things like he saw them but that was that. And the other one is, well, imagine your worst day, the worst things you had to do, the worst PT (physical training), and the worst training day; the worst of everything all rolled into one. David would be the guy who'd come through that day with some sort of obnoxious motivation and make you laugh. He could pop off a few lines and turn the whole day around. That was the best thing about him. Whatever he became a part of, things just got better." Doc took an audibly deep breath before continuing. "Funny. My God, that kid was so funny. But he was nice. He was gregarious, a very loving, sincere Marine. That's what grabbed me about him. I was 26 years old out there, and he was 21. He'd grown up a completely opposite life from what I had. And we would have talks; a lot. I mean, he'd have concerns about one thing or another but he'd always talk things out."

"David was smart, very smart actually. He was probably one of those kids who was closest to knowing everything, but was humble about it. He did what he was told, shut up when he had to shut up and do what he had to do. He'd actually make everything enjoyable for everybody else who happened to be around." Doc Clemons couldn't say enough good things about his friend. "We got close fast. We'd horse around and I mean, wherever David was, I wanted to be around him. It was a love. I loved that guy, and everything that happened that day, well, I mean, that was horrible for everybody."

"As far as wearing emotions on his sleeve? David was one of those guys who was cool and controlled. As far as knowing anything about him? Well, David had to pick you, actually. Most definitely on certain issues, in certain times, he'd come up and talk, like about a girlfriend at home and what he was going to do. Not ever in a million years would anyone be able to pick up on anything, unless he brought it up. I can't recall a time any situation where any of us were just sitting around talking about like, 'What's up with Baker?'"

"David was the kind of guy who just wanted to make everything better, including being a better person himself. He'd do everything possible, anything and everything all day. I mean, even if it was something simple like going to smoke a cigarette. He'd make that seem like it was something essential he just had to do to make it a better day. Ninety-nine percent of the guys left the Corps. David just wanted to continue to better his life, to excel. I mean, he didn't even know. He just wanted to do whatever he had to do to improve himself. He was set; keep doing right. Do the right thing. And you can bet that whatever it was that he would have ended up doing in life, he would have done his best."

"The rest of us have carried on with our own lives. As far as what David would be doing right now, I believe he'd probably be in school. I mean, if he didn't already have his Bachelor's Degree in something, he'd be right there and if not college, then some sort of technical school. Whatever he had planned for his future, he'd been doing it and would still be making people laugh along the way." Doc paused, resuming the conversation in an audibly softer voice. "You could be one of those people who thinks you're the biggest badass in all the world and here'd come David. He'd say something and you couldn't help but crack a smile."

"Patrol Base Brannon; what was a day was like there? Well, you'd wake up, get your gear on, have chow step off on patrol for six to eight hours. You'd have checkpoints, police the area, and check on the locals. When you were done with patrol, you'd come back, take off your gear, get some water, go to chow, kick off your boots, lay down to get some rest and when the next group went out, you'd go on watch. Nobody liked being on post. Even if it was your turn to go on, David would come over to help make the situation more tolerable."

"Night patrols weren't that different. And fire fights, well soon even those became regular. Locals would come to the base and complain. You could tell why the country was in the shape it was. I mean, for the most part, the ANA (Afghan National Army) was made up of men who were just fighting for; well… it was frustrating if nothing else. I mean, it definitely showed in the way they would maneuver on us. They'd know how we were going to counter even before we maneuvered. They're horrible shots, completely undisciplined. They had no uniformity, no real training about them. It made it hard for us to do our work, believe it or not."

"One incident I remember David involved in," Doc Clemons took pause again "—the Taliban know our (Marines) ROE. [12] On many occasions, they'd start randomly shooting at us because they didn't think we'd shoot back. Well, one time we had an opportunity to shoot back and in the process, some camels got shot. When all was said and done, I asked David, 'You all right?' and all he said was, '*I shot a camel.*' Doc Clemons laughed.

"We were never spooked by the ANA (Afghan National Army) who worked with us. We were briefed very early about the potential, that ours was not to not trust them, not to turn our back on them. We were certainly made aware of it. We weren't just looking at people approaching base, either. I mean, we kept our eyes on the guys with us and I know there were a few places that had taken casualties because of ANA's. One day you could be eating breakfast with them and the next day those same guys could be spraying AK's." Daniel paused. "The day David died, a couple of ANA's took casualties.

When everything happened with David, they saw we were no different from they were."

"The day he died saw us on a two-day mission that involved everybody being spread out across our AO (area of operation). From the starting line, we pushed forward, looking for anything and everything. It was a full-fledged sweep of this area. We'd went completely across this one area in its entirety looking for ANYTHING; drugs, weapons, insurgents, etc. so there was a whole bunch of us out there. David was point, so he was a little further ahead of the rest of us. It was a good sweep and so we set down for the night. Morning came, we were all feeling good so we got on line again and started pushing back essentially the same way we'd come in the night before. I didn't see David too much but it was back at the last cache we found. We were talking and joking and I was checking on everybody. We were just talking about the compound the night before when we come up on this area we'd taken contact at a number of times previously. It never failed; we were always getting shot at in this area. That day, the ANA took casualties first. We had EOD (explosive ordinance disposal) with us and they sent out their little robot to check for more explosives. Keep in mind, their little robots could only scan just so many feet aside the doors they went in. The ANA knew about this blind spot and the Taliban knew too. So EOD, they called this one area clear, and one of the ANA's stepped on a pressure plate. (The IED was in the wall.) The other ANA got peppered with shrapnel from head to toe. They started hollering for a Doc so I go springing over there. There were no real life-threatening injuries, just shrapnel so I took care of them and called for evac."

"The birds (helicopters) came in and we sent the ANA off. Everybody chilled, collected their wits. I mean, we were almost back to Brannon. We'd pushed 10-15 meters maybe (25-35 yards) and ended up by these two little hills off the side of the road. First, know this," Clemons paused gravely. "We NEVER got complacent. I mean, I'll brag on these guys until the day I die. But anyway, we'd just come through that area the night before. There were people all over the place; kids playing, I mean, all the things we were used to seeing. Staff Sergeant Cameron told David to take has wand out (metal detector) and sweep the area."

"I can remember the conversation that was going on, everybody in the patrol. I remember looking at David. He'd taken his detector out and was testing it. I couldn't have been more than 50 feet away from him. I started to turn but before I could complete the turn, there was another explosion. And I knew. I couldn't breathe. This explosion was louder. I yanked off my gear, got knocked to my knees. Yenowine rolled to the ground. Then I saw this cloud; sky-high," Doc paused. "— and I remember seeing what I saw come from that cloud. In training, there's certain things you know, things you realize. I knew whoever it was I had seen, I knew they were dead. So I start looking around, yanking off the rest of my gear, telling everybody to freeze. I yelled to Yenowine, then I saw that cloud moving off and observed Santoro and Cameron covered in blood. We'd just had an IED go off less than 30 yards from us then this one happened. So the immediate thought on my mind was 'Are there more?'"

"German went sprinting past me and I was thinking, 'Oh my God. Don't hit another one, don't hit another one.' I'd used up a lot of my supplies after the first IED went off to aid the ANA's. I didn't think I had enough medical gear to take care of Cameron and Santoro. They were both injured seriously; shrapnel, they were bleeding messes. German turned around and asked, 'Who was that?' In my mind at that moment, I thought it was this one other guy, but Santoro spoke up, 'I think its Baker.' German got a little emotional and I'm sitting there studying the situation. I mean, I had two men who needed immediate treatment, and I needed German. I told him, 'I need you, I NEED you.' I yelled for him to get the Corpsmen from the other trucks."

"They cleared the area and we treated the patients; patched them up and got them out of the vicinity and called the birds (helicopters). As the medic, it was my responsibility to go up to David. I asked the EOD guys if they had a clear path to him. They told me there was no guarantee it was clear, but I had to go, no matter what. I figured, 'To hell with it' and walked straight to him. When I saw the bottom of his cross (the tattoo on his back), I knew for sure it was him."

After a lengthy pause, Clemons continued his narrative. "Some sergeant came out to tell me we had to get David up, get him out of there and they'd brought a litter over. I mean, there was nothing I could do. I started getting all choked up but I had to go get things done. David was covered in dust," Doc's voice lowered to almost a whisper. "—everything you can imagine after stepping on an IED, that's what was before me. There's no picture to paint. I remember telling David, 'I'm sorry, man. I'm so sorry. I love you."

"We got David to the bird. I remember these other guys going into the area with black bags. This other Corpsman wanted me to use those bags for David. All I could think of was how I wanted to break this guy's neck. 'Are you out of your fucking mind?' He wanted to recover David's body and place it in one of those bags in front of everybody." Doc Clemons grew completely silent. "After the bird was gone, the guys had a hard time pulling themselves together. I never had to take care of a friend who'd been so badly taken from this world. The worst part of it all was that even after the explosion, we still had to finish clearing those houses. We still had a mission to complete."

"Everybody knew we'd taken a casualty. They were all in the worst kind of suspense. Our man Hall took control of the situation. Out of all the officers I've seen, this man was the shit. He pulled us together. We had a job to finish but nobody wanted to go point. Everybody was terrified. All I could think about was the fact David was gone."

"There was an irate guy from that village, complaining about security. As it turned out, he was the only guy with medicine in the area, so he was like a priority to keep safe. He could only tell us so much though. And whatever he told us, he would also tell the ANA. But we were like, 'Come on. You couldn't tell us there was an IED right there? No saying 'Hey, you need to be careful?' We were all so angry."

"That day, we had to push a position and another IED went off. It was like, 'Whatever' that one. We shrugged our shoulders, because at that point, it didn't seem to matter."

"We eventually got back to base. Everybody that was on the push that day ended up convening at our base. I heard Steve Aragon, and things all started to sink in. I was feeling sick. Of all the people this could have happened to, why did it have to be the one who brought life to this world? There I was, still covered with blood, David's blood. I remember thinking how that was all I had left of my buddy. I was trying to keep strong, I didn't let loose at that point. Everybody was upset; it affected everybody so deeply. The rest of the day, well, it was what it was. They briefed us and we were all there for one other. It wasn't until that night when I laid in my cubby space just looking up at the sky. 'David. I'm so sorry. I know you couldn't look through our paths, our lives, you've seen all the things I've done. I hope you understand I loved you, and couldn't do anything for you.' I cried and cried as quietly as I could."

"I talked to counselors after I got back home; talking to professionals, have the PTSD claim, talked about all the things I've lived through in my life. When I first talked to these people about this stuff, they were like 'You talk like all of this is a normal thing.' Then I explained what my life was like as I was growing up. I told them, 'I have an entire battalion of Marines you can ask to verify all of this." Doc's voice trailed in thought.

"Captain Hall approached and told me David's mom wanted to talk to me. I'll never forget in training when some petty officer told me, 'If you guys ever have to tell a parent how their child died; one day you're going to have to do exactly that.' And here I was. I remember sitting there that day he said that thinking, 'That would so suck.'"

"Mama B. (Baker's mom) only had so much patience. What I ended up telling her was, 'Your son did not suffer.' I told his brother Mark exactly how it went down. Laurie wanted details, exact details of what happened that day." Doc paused again. "Next to losing David like that, having to tell Mama B. about her son was the hardest thing I've ever done in my life."

"The IED David hit was well off the road, in a random spot. Had David stopped three feet shorter and never took another step, he would've found it with his detector. We got back to base and started thinking, 'We should have done this, and we should have done that.' But these guys knew what they were doing. This bunch were shit-hot Marines, every last one of them."

"Something like this; people can try to imagine, but unless a person has been there, they will never get it. That's the difference between feeling and knowing it."

"One of the first times I came home on leave, we went out. Well, it just so happened that on the news was some story about Afghanistan and there this guy at the bar who just would not shut up. So I turned to him and asked, 'Have you ever been in the military?' He said, 'No.' and I just stared him down. He just didn't understand, and he never would."

"I remember one time, David was writing a letter; it was a letter for when he was going to die. 'What are you doing? You're not going to die. Are you serious?' I mean, David was fearless. Overall, just like people say; 'The good die young.' When people have served their purpose, that's just it. So many people thought so much of one guy; David Baker."

"You know, I didn't join the military until I was 23. I wasn't going to connect with any of these kids; I didn't want to mix with anybody. I thought, 'Oh, these young punks think they're tough. I got nothing to relate with them.' But I did get close with these guys. Would I go back? If you gathered all the guys from that company? I sure would; in a heartbeat, even the guys I didn't get along well with. I'd give my life for every last one of them. David was the gift; just put that out there. Baker was a gift."

"One particular story I think I should share; his birthday. We were messing with him for like a week we were all going to beat the shit out of him when his birthday rolled around. Well, I'm a big guy. So when we'd start razzing with each other, he'd be like, '*Oh Doc. I'm sorry, I'm sorry.*' For his birthday, we tried to get some locals to make him a cake."

"Well, I'm chillin' in my own little space. I mean, I had tarps and blankets and boxes all set up around my cot. David pops by all nonchalant and asks, '*What're you up to?*' It instantly clicked, I mean, I knew what he was up to. 'There are only so many places you can hide.' and he says, '*Shut up, Dude. You got a cigarette?*'"

"Now, I had asked for some Berry Blue Typhoon Hawaiian Punch mix from back home. I had no big gift to give him for his birthday so I gave him my last five berry blue typhoon mixes. '*Oh man, you didn't have to give me anything.*' About that time, everybody comes in and are like, 'Happy birthday' all sweet and stuff. What they ended up doing, since they couldn't get him a cake, they bought boxes of cake mixes and stacked them up a certain way and put matches on top.' '*You guys are idiots*' was all Baker could say."

"Yenowine was a big dude, too, who'd whine about things on occasion and David would rag on him. So this one time, we were out in the Mohave Desert doing night training, and all of us are in this one vehicle. I seem to remember, well, I don't remember exactly what happened but I seem to recall hearing David say something along the lines of '*I can smooth roads. I am God and I can smooth roads.*' to Yenowine. Then he egged Yenowine by saying '*Okay Yenowine? Okay?*'" Well, there sat me and Vasquez, too and I looked at Vasquez who was laughing. So David comes to this little cliff-hill and he stopped all hard. Yenowine was like, 'What the hell?' and David was just like, '*O-kay.*' Something hit Yenowine in the mouth and we were all laughing by that time. So here comes German all serious. He was hollering at all of us, 'Get the fuck out of the truck. We are going to Afghanistan and I don't trust YOU and I don't trust YOU…' Yenowine looked at David and was like, 'Wait until we get back.' David was looking at Yenowine and popped off, '*What are you going to do? Nothing, that's what*'."

"If there was one thing the world should know about Baker, it would be the fact he was the type of person everybody loved, the type of person who treated others right. He was the young man who could show that there would always be more. Baker wasn't the guy who didn't know what he was going to do or be. He was going to continue being the great person he already had proven himself to be. The world is definitely a darker place without him. If could still be here, he'd be telling everybody, '*It happens. I want you all to be happy.*' He was one wonderful brother, a wonderful friend. Just a great guy; a good, good, man." Doc Clemons took another deep breath before continuing. "It's not that I like talking about this stuff. But I like talking about David. I don't remember a time when I was around him that I wasn't smiling."

—JAMESON O'CONNELL, USMC—

"We were all stationed together at Camp Pendleton with the 1/5. Ours was just a bunch of guys who just happened to get placed together when East Coast got put in with West Coast. It was by chance I got stationed with Baker." O'Connell paused in reverie. "I would say the first thing anybody noticed about him was his sense of humor. Before I knew him as a friend, I knew him as the guy who could turn bad situations into good ones. He was hilarious, the guy everybody liked."

"David Baker; bubbly, compassionate and caring. You have to understand something. When you are actually in the Corps, it's not cool to be all 'gung-ho' and 'Semper Fi' about things, especially in Infantry. But David, he didn't care what people thought. He was proud of everything he said and did."

O'Connell knew everybody was being asked the same standard set of questions about Baker. When he was asked about David's most memorable or outstanding attributes, this is what he had to share. "One of the most obvious things about Baker was the love he had for his family. We'd be out on field ops and everybody'd be calling their girlfriends or wives, and I'd hear David talking to his mom or his sisters." O'Connell paused in thought. "Another thing would be his passion about God. We'd stay up late talking about God, making us all re-examine our own lives. David always wanted to do right. He lived by God. I'd say his faith was definitely important to him."

"We all had ink, I mean some had more than others but David," O'Connell paused. "There were two tattoos he had that stand out in my mind; a huge cross on his back and the script that he had on his abs; FAMILY. Faith on his back and his family in front of him. That said a lot about who he was."

"David wasn't the kind of guy who showed when he was having a bad day. It was more like when any of the rest of us was in a mood or complaining about one thing or another, he'd be the one to try and get us out of that. Using all those adjectives I told you, he'd pull us all up. It was so natural he would be the one who'd try to bring us up out of our situations."

'What do you think David would be doing today?'

"I only knew David from our time in the Corps, but I know he'd want to be a good example of whatever group he represented. No matter what he did, I know he would change people's thoughts or perceptions. But whatever he'd be doing, he'd been doing it back in Ohio for sure with his family."

Talking about Patrol Base Brannon, O'Connell described what a 'day in the life of' often consisted of. "We had about 18 hours of patrol rotation. The thing that grabbed most of our time was taking watch. About twice a day, you'd climb a tower and stand up there for two hours and do all the things you'd do like radio checks and stuff. We'd find time to work out, hang out; we didn't have Internet out there—so we mostly slept, patrolled or stood watch. The main things we did as a group were play Risk or Poker. I even read some girly books, you know, the 'Twilight' series?" O'Connell laughed.

"I was on radio watch the day it happened. Their group was coming back from a two-day mission. When they were about 1-1/2 klicks (a thousand to fifteen hundred meters) away, a bomb exploded. We didn't know what was going on at first but as it turned out, that explosion was some Afghan soldiers stepping over an IED placed in a wall. We were all relieved none of our guys had been hurt but saddened by the injuries some of our ANA members received. Staff Sergeant Cameron reported in, mission was complete. Seconds after that, we heard and saw another explosion go up. Myself and another Marine who was on post, well our hearts just dropped. We didn't know what to think at the time. Then we heard there was a guardian angel."

"When they announced the names of their wounded, I transmitted their radio calls to other camps. Helicopters had been called to came in and pick everybody up. We still had no word who the KIA was. We were simply told we had two hurt and one KIA. For the next hour, we were speculating, thinking, and imagining. An hour later, they all come into camp with the grimmest look on their faces. I asked who the KIA was and that's when we were told. 'You don't know?' and we were like, 'No.' 'It was David.' The news rippled through the camp. I almost didn't believe it." O'Connell stopped speaking for a moment.

"Their patrol returned three men short. Nobody talked for the next few hours. Another group was coming in so I went out to let them know something bad had just happened so they wouldn't all be coming in laughing and carrying on. As Marines, we only had a moment to grieve. We had to carry on. Baker would have wanted it that way. So that's what we did."

"A memorial service was held a week later at our platoon's main base. We showed up and split into groups. We'd all been brought back together. It was like a mini-reunion; minus David. That was a tough moment listening to Roll Call and hearing David's name called out; the 21-gun salute was like the crowd's breath was being taken away with every shot fired. Then we lined up to pass by the memorial that was set up."

O'Connell paused, emotion apparent in every word. "That memorial was one of the most meaningful things in my life."

It had already been several years since the event of Baker's death and the majority of his Marine and Naval brothers had returned to the States and completed their military obligation. When asked if David's death still affected him today, O'Connell shared the following. "I actually have my own office and have a picture of David on the wall. I think about him at least once a day, and wonder about what things he'd be doing if he were still around. I still call and talk to a lot of the guys from the Corps. There's not a conversation we have that we don't talk about him. It's more out of happiness than mourning though. David would want it that way, for us to have joy in our lives."

"I look at everything and value life even more. There were twelve guys on our base and it could have been any one of us. David wanted to lead the way and protect us. He wanted to be 'that' guy."

"There was never a person who David came into contact with, nobody he encountered who didn't like him. There wasn't a single person; not an old Marine, not a new Marine, no matter who they were, who could ever say a bad word about him." O'Connell spoke emphatically. "One thing the world needs to know. No matter who you are or where you come from, there will always be people like David who love, who care. David was a prime example of a common misconception. Yes, he was a Marine, and yes, he was tough. But he didn't let that change him. He was still a kind and caring man who just happened to be part of the toughest group of guys in the world."

—MICHAEL JONES-RITTER, USMC—

"David is somebody who needs to be remembered and talked about..."

"I met David when I first got to fleet (the 1/5) in January 2007. The first impression he made on me? He was a real personable kind of guy. I liked him a lot. David was the kind of person that made the more difficult things we had to go through a little less harsh. He actually made them fun. You could even go so far as to say that David was the comic relief."

Asking this former Marine about attributes David possessed, he revealed emphatically, "He was real. David was very passionate in what he believed and he always stood by those beliefs. He was never the vulgar type, but instead was a very respectable, stand-up guy. He was caring, passionate, understanding. David was one of those people who had a lot of empathy for the next guy. He was always willing to help someone, always had the right words to say. Myself, I found it really easy to talk to him about things going on in my life and talked with him quite a bit. He never passed judgment."

"I don't want to say David was one for wearing his emotions on his sleeve. I think he struggled with it sometimes though. I mean, there were moments he might have wanted to let it all out, so to speak but from what I know and saw, he was always reserved. He was really good at harnessing his emotions."

As was asked of all of David Baker's fellow Marines and Corpsman, the question about what things were important to David was presented to Michael. Responding without the least bit of hesitation, he revealed the following. "First and foremost would be God and then his family. Next would be his fellow Marines. Baker had his priorities straight. I don't know, you might say that was walking the right path."

I asked this Marine what a typical day was like in Afghanistan. "I was all over the place when I was over there; Brannon, Jaker, the Mansion. No day was what you might call typical. The one thing you had to come to terms with, had to grip the reality of was that you could die at any moment. So over there, it went day by day. You were literally walking in the footprints of the guy in front of you. We had no set schedule. Every day was the same but you did it all a little differently. You didn't want routine." After a brief pause, Jones-Ritter added, "When we first got over there, it didn't seem like so many IED's (improvised explosive devices) were being used. Then they started going off more and more frequently and well…" He paused. "There was just no way to know. They got close."

Questions about the day his brother Marine lost his life were next on the list of questions asked of Jones-Ritter. "That day, we'd went out on this major platoon op. What we did was basically set security for David's squad to push through. Everything had happened and how we found out about it was this one Corporal came in as we were taking care of our weapons after the patrol. He just put it out there; 'Baker's gone.' I sat there a minute, absorbing this information, trying to take it in. At first I couldn't comprehend what he had just said. I mean, there we all were, just finished this push we had to do. We were almost going home. Up to that point, we had all been through a lot and were getting ready to get out of there." Michael hesitated briefly before continuing. "I still have a hard time thinking about how it happened."

"I went to both Roll Calls, the one in-country and the one at Pendleton. David wasn't the only Marine we lost but still to this day, I can't believe it happened. I wanted to think it was all a dream. I still have a lot of feelings. I wonder sometimes, out of all of us there, why him? He was one of those guys I would have jumped on a grenade for."

"The night before they went up there to clear, we had been out at the same location. An informant had told us the Taliban were having a big meeting that night. I mean, the same place David and his squad walked through, we had went through the night before. There weren't any IED's there."

"I know we were Marines, and we knew there was a war going on. But myself, I just didn't expect to lose a friend like that. It wasn't long after that incident that I got out of the Corps. I got myself into some trouble..." Michael paused deep in thought. "And I'm still struggling. That event, losing David, really defined who I am today. The loss of his life affects my own life more than I want it to. We all knew the possibilities, what could happen. There was a lot of sacrifice in what every one of us did."

There were many more stories that could be shared, but Michael Jones-Ritter chose to share several occasions that seemed to embody who David was to many if not all his fellow Marines. "I remember one night; it was actually the Marine Corps Ball out in Vegas. Baker and I had gone out and man, I got hammered. I couldn't make it back to the hotel so David literally carried me back. That was just one occasion, one thing that happened that made our friendship grow. I mean, we were Marines and that made us brothers, but things that happened when we'd go hang out, those were the things that really made that bond grow."

"There was another time in Afghanistan, one night we were sitting up really late, just sitting outside talking under the stars about things like what we were going to do when we got back to the States, unwinding I guess. David was a really great guy to talk to. If you were feeling down about anything, he was the guy you could go to. You'd feel a lot better after talking with him."

"One thing about David; he wouldn't let emotion get the better of him in any kind of argument. He'd use logic. Anything he said, you could always take to the bank. He wouldn't just give you an answer; he would explain the logic behind the answer. You couldn't argue with David anyway, he'd always win."

"I don't want him to be forgotten. David Baker was a real stand-up kind of guy. He was the icon of selflessness. He was one of our Marines who paid the ultimate price, and that's something that shouldn't ever be taken for granted."

—IAN PLUMLEE, USMC—

"When did I meet David? We had mutual friends and ran into each other a few times, but we didn't hang out until our first deployment. We were on guard on ship and assigned post together a lot. Since there wasn't much else to do, we'd start shootin' the shit and got to know each other in the process." Plumlee drew in a deep breath before continuing. "He wasn't like a lot of the guys I ran into. David was more forthcoming; he opened himself up to people. Not everybody, especially in the Marines, open themselves up that way. It was good to run into somebody like that."

When Plumlee was asked to identify some of Baker's most outstanding or most memorable attributes, his response was swift. "*All* of them. David had so many great qualities. He was accepting of other people. He was funny, real sarcastic, open-minded, and sensitive under the surface." Plumlee's voice trailed off. "I was engaged at the time, had a girl back home who was going to have a baby. I wasn't going to be there for that and, well, David was one of the few guys I could sit down and talk to about it. He didn't just blow it off. He paid attention, took things to heart. He genuinely tried to help. That's the kind of guy he was."

"They held a memorial for him while we were still deployed but I wasn't able to make that one. I got to pay my respects once we were back stateside at Pendleton. They held a memorial service for all the guys we'd lost in Afghanistan.

That's when the full reality of the loss of four fine men truly struck me." Plumlee waited patiently for the next question. "I hadn't seen David much after we deployed. When I found out he'd been killed, it put a dark cloud over everything; every one. David wasn't the only one we lost on that deployment," Plumlee paused. "—but he and another Marine Justin Swanson, they were two close friends. I broke down a little, sure. And their losses still affect me every day. Just the fact that, regardless of the reality of the danger, you never think it's going to happen to you. The fact is, though, that it's always a very real possibility. But it's a job, you know; join the Marines, serve your country, and get out. It's all cool; that's how we saw it. But to have the loss of people to contend with, especially people so close and so young," Plumlee's voice waivered ever so slightly. "Yes, it definitely affects you."

"As much as everybody in the Corps tries to give off that 'I don't give a fuck attitude', David was one of those guys who held his friends in high regard. His family and his Marine brothers came first, most definitely. The friends in the military, those are friends you're going to have forever; no matter where they get off to after they're out." Ian paused as he thought about his friend. "David was meticulous in everything he did. He liked being recognized as a hard worker and the dedicated Marine that he was. He was most definitely a very good person to call your friend, especially in the Marines."

"When everything happened, I was quite a ways away and didn't hear about it immediately. You know, they don't put the information out there very quickly. I was at post standing guard and the guy who came out to relieve me; he was a younger, newer guy. He said, 'Lance Corporal Baker was killed by an IED.' I'm sure he didn't know who David was, thinking about it now, or there's no way he could have said it so nonchalantly. I thought it had to be some other Baker. I was in that stage of denial and refused to accept the fact it could actually be David; until it was confirmed later that day. That's when it hit me."

To better understand the environment these Marines were fighting in on a day to day basis, I asked Plumlee to give me an opinion about progress the Marines were making overseas. "We weren't fighting an organized military, they followed no rules. You didn't know from day to day who was going to be your enemy. One day you would be invited into someone's home, the next day they you be trying to kill you. It reminds me of something General James Mattis said, 'Be polite, be professional, but have a plan to kill everybody you meet.' You have to acknowledge that. You have to be able to do your job. I mean, you always got to keep a healthy fear in the back of your mind, that's called situational awareness, and it's what's going to keep you alive so you can get back home."

"I remember meeting up with David one time at the bar. It was interesting to actually just hang out with him outside of our military work environment. When we did, it was a blast. He was always looking to put a smile on people's faces, even if it was at his own expense. He could laugh at himself, always found humor in even the worst of situations. You could always rely on David to break the tension with some smartass, sarcastic joke."

"David was kind of above the rest. He was proud of his family, where he came from." Plumlee drew in a slow, deep breath. "He definitely was the type to let his mind be known. He was tactful about it though. Even the higher-ups couldn't hold back their smiles. When you can positively affect people who aren't supposed to be affected at all? That says a lot about a man. It said everything about David."

—MIKAH JAMES, USN—

"I've just finished doing fourteen years. Was a full-blown E-5 and they put me out (2013). But I was Senior Corpsman for Weapons Company in 2008 when I checked into the 1/5 right before deployment on WestPac. I met David out on the smoke deck. He walked up with a group of guys; Kyle Skeels, Matt German and Terry Silken. When the three of them walked up, we clicked right off the bat. David was the guy who could always put a smile on your face. If anything was ever bothering you, he'd come up and make you think outside the box, turn things around."

"David was a crazy, outgoing, and fun-loving guy who was hard to knock down. He was an all-round good guy. But on the other hand, if he had something to say, he'd come right out and say it. He didn't hold anything back."

James was asked what he thought was most important to David. Without hesitation, he answered, "Family. And friends. He always put them first."

"When he got killed, I was at Balboa doing CT tech work. I got the message from Silken's mother. She texted me that Baker was KIA. A lump formed in my throat immediately. I mean, Baker was my brother." James lowered his voice and continued. "It wasn't long after that I happened to be scrolling through my phone and I stopped at David's name. 'That's a number I'll never be able to call again.' His death still affects my life. David was the first of my friends/Marines who were KIA. He wasn't just a Marine, he was my brother."

"I was his Corpsman at one time. It was MY job to take care of him. I held that on my shoulders the whole time. I kept thinking, 'I could have done this' or 'I could have done that'. German was there and he told me, 'When I came up on him, there was nothing you could've done.' I felt responsible."

"I remember one time in Dubai," Mikah paused. "David could close his left eye like he could only see out of one eye. When the waitress walked up to take our drink order, David closed that eye. It was all we could do to keep from laughing. When she walked away, we all busted out laughing."

—DENNIS HOLMES, USMC—

"Other than the Marines, his biggest love was God and his family." (October 07, 2012)

"When I first met Baker, it was October of 2006 in SOI. Being a mortar man was an easy job—so we were told. It entailed throwing rockets down tubes then having to set a base plate, drop a barrel in the base plate, and getting the gun up. The gunner's duty was to input data into a sight and the assistant gunner's job was to get the gun on aiming stakes set out by the ammo man. So it was like, 'Hey, that sounds like fun.'"

"At first, I thought Baker was an asshole. He was funny, but he was a dickhead at the same time. One time, me, David and a few other guys want out to San Diego. Crossing outside of crosswalks was a big deal out there then. David went to cross outside a walk and I told him, 'Don't do it man.' He goes ahead and crosses outside the walk against the light and gets a jaywalking ticket. He was mad as hell."

"We went to TGI Fridays to drink and in the process, we met these girls. Nothing happened at Fridays so we go our separate ways. As we were leaving, we met up with those same girls. They were going to a cigarette party and had all these different kinds of cigarettes on them so they let us try a few. David gets done with smoking what he was going to smoke of his cigarette and pitched what was left. That cigarette didn't just land on the ground. It hit a cop's foot, the same cop who'd written him a ticket for jaywalking earlier." Holmes laughed before continuing. "David wasn't a super serious kind of guy; until we got to Afghanistan."

"My overall impression of David? He was funny. He could do this character called 'Salad Fingers' really well. There's videos on You Tube showing what that is." Dennis continued. "He was a family man, first and foremost. He cared about his family. He told me a story about a guy putting one of his sisters into the trunk of a car one time. I guess he went and found the guy and beat the hell out of him, too for doing what he did." Holmes finished his thoughts. "Second would be God. That and making people laugh. He was good at it. You couldn't stay mad at him forever. That was impossible."

"The last conversation we had was probably when we were all talking about how bad we wanted to get back home. (We were in Afghanistan and I was just visiting his base dropping off some supplies and mail. He was at PB Brannon while I was at PB Sullivan aka 'The Mansion.' We talked about food and women..."

"Let me tell you about this time in Kuwait. It was our first deployment and we were playing hackeysack. David came up and hit me in the head with a bottle of ice, almost knocking me out. So I got a couple of bottles and was going to beat his head in. I mean, I was mad. So he ran and kept saying. '*Holmes don't do it.*' It was in my mind, 'If you kill him, you'll get in trouble. If you hit him, you'll get in trouble.' I finally cooled off and stopped chasing him."

In describing how a day ran for them in Afghanistan, Holmes continued. "We'd wake up. Ready for morning patrol, come back, chill out, and go out on night. Every four days, you'd be on a fire watch. Every eight hours, you did a four-hour post. Standing Post means basically standing guard for an allotted amount of time making sure nobody is trying to get in or, if we received fire, to determine where it came from."

Dennis shared another story about how they passed time. "It was so hot outside. There was this big concrete pillar we'd throw water on and the water would just evaporate immediately. It was like 154F over there during the day and could drop to 34F. The hottest day was probably when we first got there and walked off the plane. The coldest? No bull, that was October 1st. (Baker's birthday.) We woke up and, 'BAM!' it went from 150F the day before to 34F. It was terrible. Nobody had their cold weather gear ready."

When asked about the day Baker died, Dennis Holmes turned quiet before answering. "I was on fire-watch and saw the explosion. They said 'Heaven had a new angel.' I guess I didn't want to believe it was true. David was one of the best guys there. I mean, you don't want anybody to be the one, but I just couldn't see David being the one."

"They wouldn't let me go to the memorial over there (in Afghanistan) but I did go to the one at Pendleton. That's when I first met his family. It was about a week after that we all pitched in money to have his dress blues put into a shadow box. We presented it to Mama B."

When asked about Arlington, Holmes gave a little snicker. "October 2009. I wanted to go to David's Memorial service but my ex-wife wanted me to go to a wedding. Long story short, I got smashed and ended up getting emotional. My wife left the next day (and I was glad too, except she took my dog, the only thing I wanted.) Baker was the first guy I knew personally who died but the following month, we lost another guy."

"I have a story to share. It was Presidents Day in 2007, and we'd all planned to go to San Francisco. I decided to make it into a road trip. David predicted I was going to wreck my car. Well, he was right. I did have a wreck; ended up hitting a semi at 80mph. I called David and was like, "Dude. I'm not gonna make it." All he said was, '*You got in a wreck, didn't you?*' My car was totaled; nothing left, but there wasn't a scratch on me."

"David was the cool guy, the person everyone liked. Sure sometimes he went too far but like I said before, you couldn't stay mad at him. He was goofy almost all the time, but when it came down to his family or God you couldn't get even a smirk out of him. He was a great guy."

—JIMMY BERAN, USMC—

"I first met David in January or February of 2007. We came in with a group of about 30-40 people who were just sort of dropped into the platoon. I'd done West Coast school of infantry and David had gone East Coast. I can't remember who he was roommates with but that's how he and I met. He seemed like he'd be a great guy to get to know. We were roommates better than half the time we were in the unit."

"David always had a great sense of humor; just a witty guy. His jokes poked fun at people but not in a mean-spirited kind of way. And he was easy to talk to, but kind of shy at the same time." Beran grew silent as he thought about what to say next. "I know he took his faith seriously. You know, he had his book of prayers; that book was ALWAYS by his bedside." Beran paused in thought. "I remember one time, I had a rosary hanging in my car on the rearview mirror. He always seemed to have respect for that. Like if it was hanging crooked, he'd reach up and straighten it."

"You ask about the things important to him? Like I said, his faith. And he loved his family. He even had a tattoo across his abs that said 'FAMILY' in great-big letters. One time, stateside, we were all hanging out at the bars and he stopped in the middle of things to call home. I mean, I didn't know anybody our age that would do that. He was just a great guy to know; a real friendly, caring, trustworthy kind of guy to know."

"David was never one who wore emotions on his sleeve. But once you got to know him, you could tell how he was feeling about stuff. He wasn't out in the open with his feelings but you could just tell. He did a good job keeping his temper, too." Beran paused a moment. "As far as the things that mattered to him most? You could tell how much he cared for his friends and family. If I had to put any kind of order to things, I'd have to say he valued his family, his faith then his friends. I mean, David would poke fun at people sometimes, lots of times he'd be the one instigating things, but it was always in fun, never maliciously."

"We were originally in the same section of our platoon when there were only enough guys for two sections. Eventually, we got enough new people to make a third and I got moved. David stayed and because of that, we didn't get to see a whole lot of each other in Afghanistan. While we were over there, I was at a base that had this incredibly slow internet connection. It was slow but we could catch in-coming stuff about things going on back home. I remember Ohio State had lost a game and I'd mentioned this to David in passing, about how they'd lost the USC. He was like, 'How'd Nebraska do?' and he'd asked who they were going to play the following week. I think it was like Virginia Tech or something. Anyway, he told me he was sure they'd take care of them, too. Well, he was right." Beran paused in silence. "I never got the chance to rub it in because everything happened."

"David would fall asleep every night watching a movie. We'd wake up with the alarm and the stupid DVD soundtrack playing." Beran chuckled. "Here's a story I'm sure you've already heard. We were cleaning; I mean super cleaning the barracks. (Field Day.) It wasn't like a major inspection, but we were getting checked by the higher-ups. I'd broken my ankle, so I had this big cast. To take a shower, I had to have this plastic wrap on my leg. So, there's David and I and all of us all cleaning for inspection. Neither one of us wanted to clean the shower. So I offered to go in like I was taking a shower. At first, David was skeptical. *'I don't know if that's going to work.'* So I go in there and started taking my shower. They came in to inspect the barracks and of course, we got failed on stuff but David told me to stay in the shower while he fixed the stuff we'd been failed on. Well, they kept failing us. So I ended up staying in the shower for hours. One guy who'd come in to inspect us earlier that day just happened to be the one who came back and was like, 'How in the hell are you still in the shower?'"

"I was originally at Patrol Base Jaker with Charlie Company at this compound we'd taken over. David was with Alpha Company. After the first month, we'd all gone back to Camp Leatherneck to get all organized and stuff but we got split up again after that."

"The day David died started out like any other day. We'd been on morning patrol (we patrolled eight hours a day) and were sitting around relaxing before we had to go out and do it all over again. Well, we were sitting there and our squad-leader walks in and told us, 'Mohawk suffered a KIA.'" Beran paused briefly before continuing, "At that moment, I knew one of my friends had just been killed, I just didn't know who. I started running through the list of guys in my mind just thinking to myself, 'I might never see this guy or that guy ever again.' I mean I never thought about it being David. I don't remember how long it was exactly before I found out but eventually, the sergeant came back in and he told us who it was." Beran stopped. "It was one of the worst feelings in my life."

"There was only one other guy with me at that base who knew David. We kind of—" Jimmy trailed off. "I just started pacing around because I didn't know how to take it. It sucked because everybody in sections One and Two had each other. Our third section, the one I was in, was full of newer guys. They knew who David was but didn't know him. I felt kind of alone in dealing with this. I was numb inside."

"The Memorial was held at our base. We were at a compound that was perfect for a base. It had 20 ft. high walls a couple of feet thick with an iron gate out in front. It had three separate buildings and was just so huge inside. This was where we had the whole platoon and the Memorial Service for David. People gave speeches; you know, like the battalion and brigade commanders, and General Nicholson. We had a Roll Call ceremony there, too. That was very nice; horribly depressing, though. David deserved all of that and then some."

Beran was asked how David's death affected his life today. With an emotionally controlled voice, Beran shared his answer. "I think about him a lot. Earlier this year. I went to Arlington. That was nice. It was moving. I miss him a lot, all the time. We're all out now, and even though he'd been living in Ohio, it sucks that I can't message him or—" He paused again to gather his thoughts. "His memory is still here, in the hearts and minds of everybody who knew him."

—MATT DEAN, USMC—

"The first time Baker and I met was in SOI at the 1/5. We were out doing a field op, actually." Dean paused in thought before continuing. "The guys in Weapons Company always hung out together. David was a real friendly guy, and talkative, too. He was never intimidating. You know, we'd all go out to different places and here was Baker; he was just so tight with everyone. Weapons was a tight company, anyway." Dean paused again. "For example, when I got married (I just had my wedding not too long ago.) about twenty of the guys came into town for it. I mean, I was older than most of them, so a lot of them called me Grandpa Dean. But we're all still close. And David?" Dean paused. "He was the one who was going to make you laugh, for sure."

"In describing David, I'd have to say first of all he was the guy who'd have your back, no matter what. I can tell you for a fact he'd have it in a heartbeat. He was the kind of guy who was real loyal to his friends. But another great thing about him was he could make people laugh, and he was good at it. Baker was a clown. I kind of think of him as a goofy guy, you know? He was such a real good guy." Matt Dean's voice softened ever so slightly as he continued. "I can remember everything about him right up to the last time we ever talked."

"As far as being able to read David, he wasn't a real emotional guy. I mean, if he was, he hid that, unless he was pissed. (I only saw him get like that a few times.) He had it all together. I can tell you, one of the most important things to him was family. The guy loved his mom a lot, and no doubt he loved his friends."

When asked to describe what a day was like in Afghanistan, Dean responded quickly. "I wasn't with David over there but was at a post nearby. We'd stop at Brannon (David's base) all the time. Actually, the last time I talked to him was at PB Brannon." Dean paused briefly. "Your day depended on what section or squad you operated with. Our bunch operated a little differently than the rest. Lots of times when you were on post, you just did your job. You did whatever you had to get done then do it all over again the next day. When I ran with them, it was like eight days out on patrol, eight days on post. Patrols started at around 0700 depending on the kind you had. You'd get all your guys to gear up, step off on patrol, come back, and another squad would go out. We'd rotate like that. Night time, you'd get ready for fire watch. Days over there were long and boring. Most of the time, you just had a lot of time to think."

"We did a mission on 19 October-my platoon and David's squad. The day before, my platoon had kind of went through and swept that village where David was killed. We woke up the next morning, pushed through the same area, and were up at the village waiting on 81. We could see them." Dean stopped, thinking of the words he was going to say next. "Two IED's went off that day. We saw the first blast and found out it was ANA (Afghan National Army) and everything was ok. Then the second blast went off and we saw that one, too. I heard Aragon on the radio reporting everything. 'We have an angel.' You know, no names get broadcast when things like that happen. When my squad pushed back to Brannon, we found out who the angel was. O'Connell came out when we were coming in and told me. That was one sad day."

"It hurt because David was such a good guy. We'd cut through a lot together in Weapons. Like I said before, we were a tight-knit bunch; a good band of brothers. When everything all went down, some of the guys were tremendously affected. I mean, they were standing right there when it happened. They had the roll call in Afghanistan, which was another sad day. Everybody was really down but we were like, 'We've got to do this for Dave.' It was around this time we knew things in country were coming to an end soon and we were all like, 'Damn. We almost made it out of here and then that happened to David." Dean fell silent.

"There was probably a big hit the day before my team was there in that area where David was killed. We'd found some wires," Matt's voice grew thoughtful. "We'd patrol those areas so much. And they'd (Afghani's) just re-route. You know, there'd be IED after IED. It was just one of those spots they liked to place IED's I suppose. The Taliban was working both sides. The people didn't know what to do. I mean they were in a bad spot."

When Dean was asked to describe a particularly memorable time about Baker, his response was "There's not just one time. We had a LOT of good times at Pacific Beach. There was this one time David jumped into the trunk of a car trying to get back on base, or this other time at the Marine Corp Ball where he jumped on my mom's back and gave her this great big bear hug, a lot of memories on ship and in the field on down time; good camaraderie. The last day I talked to him, well, they'd always run out to meet us and be shouting, 'En route! En route!' Stuff like that." Dean paused again. "Just a lot of good things to remember."

"Mine sweeping is one of those things; I was a squad-leader, and-." His thoughts were coming quickly as he answered one of the last interview questions presented. "You know, I had a tattoo done on my arm in honor of David. And I wear a bracelet every day. I know my other brothers are hurting, too."

—BRIAN MONAHAN, USMC—

"I first met David at SOI East Coast at Camp Geiger/Camp LeJeune in Charlie Company.

Nobody knows anybody at first other than the fact that we're a bunch of Marines all put together to train. For the first couple of weeks, everybody's the same. Then you break off into your sections. We all went to Weapons Company." Monahan began. "But to describe David? At first, I'd have called him one of the quiet guys. It wasn't until we were in SOI we all got to know each other." He paused. "That was on the weekends, when we all got together."

"David had a dry but witty sense of humor; very witty. For instance, if you were hanging out with him, he was like, a Grammar Nazi. I'd be talking and say 'Dan and me' and David would immediately correct me; *'Dan and I, it's Dan and I'* and he'd do it with a straight face." Monahan gave a thoughtful pause before continuing. "Obviously he was very smart, quiet, and humorous. He was a good-looking dude, too. That's David in a nutshell. And he was humble. David was humble; never obnoxious."

"He wasn't one of those guys who'd wear his emotions on his sleeve; at least I wouldn't say he was. Some might say he was but," Monahan paused. "—well, let me tell you. In 2009 when we were in Afghanistan, my truck hit an IED. When we got back to the FOB, (forward operating base) we got word David's platoon was up there. So when I walked in, a bunch of 81's come up to me all happy and, well, they'd been worried;

a little concerned when they heard about the IED. That was the last time I saw him—" Monahan's voice trailed off.

"I think about this every day, I just don't talk about it. I mean, it goes along with everything you do. When I first got out (of the Marines) a big thing was adjusting back to civilian life. You come home and step into the swing of regular life and you kind of feel like nobody appreciates shit. When you'd be home on leave, it'd be all like 'thank you' and everything. But when we got out for good, it was a whole different story. Maybe it's just from my surroundings. I don't know; adjusting back to civilian life. A lot of guys have all this anger built up inside that's made it hard to cope when they got back." Monahan paused. "Like I said, when you get out for good, everybody's singing a different tune. So coming home, guys rebel against everything and just say, 'Fuck this' or 'Fuck that' and start drinking. Shit, they just go off, and I think, 'Just go listen to some music or something,' You start thinking of all the ones who didn't come home and then wonder if they'd be wanting you to be acting that way. Well," Monahan paused again "Fuck what everybody else thinks. I'm going to do what I think David would want me to do. Now I have to follow through on this. You know what I'm saying?" Monahan asked as he explained his thoughts. "I take David's death in a way that makes me think I need to better myself, so his death wasn't for nothing. I've spoken with Mama B. about this. These guys sacrificed their lives for us and would want us to better with our lives.

"The day David died, I was in section one. Section two was going out to do a round with Baker's section. Now, when an IED goes off, you hear it through the AO. I was on watch and I heard the IED go off. The radio comes over and says, 'No casualties, everybody's okay.' That was the last I'd heard about it that night. So early next morning, we get relieved and push back to our COP (combat outpost)."

Monahan was asked where he was at the time of Bakers death. "I was up north in Bravo Company. I never went out on any patrols with David. We were unloading the truck and Mendez goes in and comes right back outside. We were all out there joking around and smiles when Mendez, another Marine came out to tell us it was a bad moment. I immediately knew we'd lost somebody. Mendez says, 'We lost Baker.' I couldn't even cry…" Monahan let his voice trail, collecting his emotions before speaking again. "I immediately thought of Dan Guider. You think of everybody you know. It didn't hit me at first; you don't want to believe it. I dumped everything and ran into the post. There's a whole platoon in there, 40 guys, and you could hear a pin drop. Dan Guider was sitting Indian style in the dirt, chain smoking. I dropped in front of Guider and just grabbed him, looked at him. All I could say was, 'Fuck, Dan. I'm sorry.' Saying sorry to Dan was as close as I could get to giving condolence. I don't think he had any tears left to cry. I just hugged him and walked away. I had to get ready for patrol."

"Usually, you just get a short brief about patrol. We'd just lost a good friend. So you know when you go out there, you're going to run into people who you don't know if they had any part of Baker's death. While sitting there in country, there was no way to console his family and we were thinking, 'Mama B. is getting the news right now.'" Monahan took pause again, the emotion fresh in his mind. "I can tell you for any Marine I've ever met, any Marine would have rathered it'd been them. Not for the fact 'I'm gonna be a hero', either. It was because Baker'd have been like, 'I want my boys to live.' That could have been any of us. He put himself out there for all of us. It was the most surreal moment of my life." Monahan sighed audibly. "But we still had to go out and do our job. There was a lot of anger on that patrol."

"When something traumatic happens in the military, your adrenaline starts rushing. After that moment, whatever that moment may be, everybody has a different vision of it. You may think something particular happened and be off from somebody else's reality. My story will be different than that of the guy standing right next to me. Dan Guider was just the first person I attached to after hearing about Baker. Dan's reaction, the expression on his face, the demeanor of his body…" Monahan seemed to be searching for his next words. "He was pale, his expression bland. There was nothing there."

"For the next couple of days after it happened, we all reminisced about Baker. We talked about everything for hours. It was the best way to cope with it."

"It was at Camp Pendleton when I first met Mama B. We all knew what was going to happen at the ceremony because we rehearsed. But when it came down to the actual event, I think that was the second most dramatic moment I've experienced." Brian took a deep breath and continued. "When they called the names of the missing; no response. I remember questioning if this was the right way to do it. But it's tradition. The moment really strikes you in the heart and that moment in time pauses. It was dark and cold; it sucked. But afterward, when we broke formation and his mom stepped up to the boots and rifle…" He paused with recollection. "I took a knee and held his dog tags. That was the first time I cried. I immediately felt the tears rushing. I stood up and went to the barracks and cried on my own. I felt at that moment, the last person Baker's mother needed to see break down was any of us."

"That night, we went out to dinner together in San Clemente. After dinner, Mama B. came outside. We were all standing out there and she shared what had happened on the home front from her side after David was killed. That got me thinking about his whole family, a whole new perspective to it all." When asked his thoughts about Baker now, Monahan responded, "Always, always every day I think how David gave his life and how his death saved people."

"We had an in-country memorial service too, before Pendleton. But everybody didn't get to go. Our platoon was upset we didn't get to that Roll Call. We couldn't leave. It was hard, but David would have understood. We still had a job to do."

Monahan had a story to share about David. "One night, we were stateside, and I'm walking back to the barracks after I'd been out drinking. As I passed the 81's barracks, there were these three guys up on the balcony. (As it turned out, it was Aragon, Carr, and Baker.) I had my hood on so they didn't know it was me. So I yelled up, 'How about you POG's go to bed? Why don't you POGs go to bed?' (POG is 'person other than grunt'. Infantry are grunts. Calling a non-infantry person a POG is offensive.) Aragon hollered down, 'I'm going to fuck you up.' He was taking the lead to come out and fight. Baker was all quiet and Carr was looking at Baker but Baker was right behind Aragon. So Carr was like, 'You've got some shit to say?' They found out it was me. "Monahan, what the fuck are you doing?' Aragon was, 'I was ready to fuck you up, man."

Brian reminisced about David a few minutes before telling about the hand he had in a fundraiser honoring his Marine brother. "I play a lot of recreational sports. One day I was thinking about how I wanted to do a fundraiser for Baker. So

I called Mama B. to get authorization. I figured the best way to do it would be as a half-and-half with Wounded Warrior Project getting one half and David's Scholarship fund getting the other. So she put me in touch with Bill Wade in Ohio and I went to City Hall in Glenn Cove, New York to get use of the athletic fields. After a bit of a run-around, I was finally given a date and put together the event in three weeks. On April 14th, 2012 we had 14 teams register for a five on five football tournament and raised $7,000 total. We had shirts made and businesses and restaurants donated things to raffle. A few guys came in from Boston and Chicago. Thank God we had good weather. People were really responsive."

—VINCENT MORALES, USMC—

"I didn't know David that well but a lot of guys in my barracks had served with him at SOI (School of Infantry). We ended up at one of the same parties in San Diego, basically friends of friends. I didn't have a lot of direct contact with him but it says something about the caliber of person he was when word of mouth preceded his reputation. David was definitely known as a fun kind of guy."

"Baker was funny as hell, absolutely hilarious. Like I said before, I didn't know him well enough to be able to tell you about things I thought most important to him but people would tell me stories about things they did over the weekends or on leave. After Baker was killed, the guys in my company reminisced about him a lot; the best parts, like how he could always lift everybody's spirits, keep everybody happy and in good moods. He was the kind of guy you wanted in your platoon. He kept everybody's moral where it needed to be."

When asked how he felt upon hearing about what happened to David, Morales continued narrating his thoughts. "You never have a normal day out there, anyway. Your heart just sinks as soon as you hear about one of your own being taken out like that." His voice grew quieter as he continued. "And to see how a bunch of Marines are affected—" His voice trailed off.

"They held a Roll Call memorial in-country. We still had our job to do, but when they held the ceremony over there, they let some of the guys who were closer to him go down to attend. I went to the one at Pendleton. That was tough, real tough. It wasn't my first roll call, either." Morales's voice changed tone again. "I didn't meet any of his family. Soon as that roll call was over, I went back to my room."

Vincent drew in a deep sigh before speaking again. "Witnessing the loss of brothers," he paused "—I try not to let it affect me, but it does. You can never get away from that. I mean, I know no matter what, we're going to lose people. It's just the nature of who we are and what we do. That's reality. We know it going in. I just never know how I'm going to react, if I'm going to be able to deal with it or not. But after Baker died, I knew for sure. It made me more aware of life. Death too, for that matter."

When asked for final thoughts, Morales had this to share. "Anybody who's gonna buy this book already knows what happened to Baker. Anybody else? They don't care. They weren't affected by his death. And that's the problem. People know all these horrible things happen over there, all these awful things are going on, but they choose not to be aware. Awareness. You can't force awareness on people here in America. People that want to know? They already know. For everybody else, well, it might only be for a fleeting moment, but then they're done. They don't see a reason to care."

—DAN GUIDER, USMC—

"Baker could be quite the Grammar Nazi. For example, if I ever said something like, 'Me and Skeels are going to San Diego', I would've been cut off at 'are going' and David would have said "*Skeels and I*." So, sorry for all the run-on sentences and bad punctuation in advance."

"I don't think anyone will ever hold a candle to David. We had a lot of fun. There's not a period in my life that will trump that at all."

"I met David at the UMA Lot at Camp San Mateo (a sub camp of Camp Pendleton.) There was David, Kyle Skeels, myself and a couple of other guys who were being sent in to be aggressors for the battalion's pre-deployment training for Weapons Company. It wasn't but within the first few minutes of meeting him he had me laughing, and I didn't stop until his death. He was always one for cracking jokes. I mean, it seemed no matter what stupidity the Battalion would throw at us, David could always lift the company's spirits. Ours was a tight company, too. There weren't any cliques."

"David's ability to make people laugh was one of his most obvious attributes. But one that probably went unnoticed (unless you spent a lot of time with him) was how much he cared for his friends and family. Making people laugh wasn't the only thing I could tell you about the guy. Besides being so funny, he was genuine, he was selfless and caring; and unforgettable."

"I remember one time when we went to Mission Beach for the weekend; I got a ticket for drinking underage. David was probably more worried about it than I was. Though you have to understand something. For civilians, an MIP (minor in possession) isn't a big deal. But the Marine Corps makes big deals out of parking tickets so an MIP to us was like an 'Oh SHIT' moment. After I got done with the cops, we went and got something to eat. Baker spent the whole time cheering me up and helping me work out a game plan for what to do about the situation at work the following Monday. We decided that saying nothing was the best policy and as it turned out, that really was. David and another friend of ours Scott Santoro went to my court date with me for moral support and the judge ended up letting me off easy with just a $35 dollar fine. Baker and Santoro ended up getting MIPs in Mission Beach a couple weeks later and we repeated the whole process with similar results. That was just the kind of person David was. He would be genuinely upset if you were and do everything in his power to make you feel better (which he was usually successful at, too by the way.)"

"Shortly after this, we deployed on the 11th Marine Expeditionary Unit. At the time, there were rumors going around about us going to Afghanistan on that deployment. I remember going to Carl Jr's (a restaurant) with David a few days before we deployed and talking about the possibility of Afghanistan. He told me point blank if we went, he didn't think he'd come back. We didn't end up going on that particular deployment, but I think he might have held on to that. I know everyone always talks about 'the guy who knew he wasn't coming back.' At the time I thought, 'C'mon man. That's bullshit.' Now I think there's some kind of truth to that."

"I think that's the thing that bothered me most; transitioning from the Marines to college. There's kids going to college on their parent's dime and don't even care. Theirs is a completely different world, where war is something they watched on TV or played on X-Box. I wish it could be made a requirement for college admissions; assign applicants the name of a twenty-something year-old killed in action and have them write a research paper on him/her. Write about who they were, what they were like, what their dreams were, what they meant to others, who their family still is; have them write something that puts a face and a person to the name."

"For all the talk that goes on in college classes about war and how terrible it is, 99% of students talking have no clue what it's all about. They discuss it in class and leave afterward, just forgetting about it. It sucks to think David died for these people and they could care less."

"As far as my impression of things important to David, that's an easy question to answer; God, family and friends. I gave David a ride back from the airport after a leave block, and we were listening to '*Landing in London*' by Three Doors Down. It's kind of a depressing song but we probably listened to it four or five times because it went with how David was feeling about being away from his family at the time. There were times he'd sit in the barracks and smell his clothes as he unpacked because "*They still smell like home*" (direct quote.) Like I told you with the MIP story, David was always there for his friends. I think that's the true mark of a Marine. The way he died was also the way he lived; always looking out for his brothers."

"David died during a clearing operation. They'd been taking fairly regular contact in their AO (area of operation) and the company decided a clearing operation needed to take place. They were hoping to find some weapons caches or try to provoke a fight. So my section (CAAT-2) and a section from CAAT-1 went to Brannon to join a squad from 81's."

"I was pumped. I mean, the last time I'd seen David was late July at FOB Geronimo before they moved to southern Nawa. (Weapons Company was spread out over the Western edge of Nawa and my platoon was in the Northwestern sector.) We'd been searching compounds for the second day and were wrapping things up. It was sometime in the late afternoon or early evening when there was an explosion about 1000 meters to our northwest. Our second radio wasn't working so we only had com (communication) with our platoon. We'd radioed our lead truck and asked if they knew anything about the explosion. They said they thought it was just a controlled detonation (common occurrence, usually blowing off IEDs found during patrols) so we thought nothing of it. Come to find out later, it'd been announced David was killed."

"So up to that point, I was oblivious to the fact anyone had been hurt, much less the fact my good friend had been killed. We got back to Brannon and I grabbed a bag of trash from the backseat to take to the burn pit, still pumped that I was going to get to go bullshit with Baker and see the rest of the 81's. I got about ten feet from the truck when O'Connell (Jamison) said he needed to talk to me. Still oblivious, I asked, 'What's up?' O'Connell told me Baker didn't make it. I was kind of like, 'What are you talking about?' and he said, 'Baker's dead.' I didn't believe it. I actually asked if he were fucking with me. It took a second to hit me, and I went back to the truck and sat by the back tire and started crying. I told the rest of my truck Baker was gone and then went into the PB. I saw all the 81's; it was quiet and no one said anything, everybody was either crying or in shock."

"My section left when it started getting dark, heading back to COP Casa Bonita. When we got back, everyone was sleeping, so we didn't wake them to tell them the news. I went to sleep and woke up a couple hours later to stand the 0400-0800 post and Brian Monahan, another friend of Baker's came up around 0600 and stood the rest of post with me. Words can't do justice to who David was. All I can say is his death deprived a lot of people of the opportunity to have David in their life."

Roll Call at Camp Pendleton: "I put the helmet on the rifle for his warrior's cross. I kind of zoned out while I was doing that. The whole ceremony was surreal. I don't think it was until after the formal ceremony when we went up and touched his dog tags that it hit me. It hurts to realize he's gone. He wanted nothing more than to finish his four years and move on with his life. The rest of us are doing just that and it was taken away from him. I think about David every day. I don't think that'll ever change for the rest of my life. I believe it's important to remember he sacrificed his future for the rest of us."

"The fact David's gone is hard for me to comprehend. It's one of those things where you sit and think 'that couldn't have happened'. They say time heals all wounds, but I think that saying also implies as time goes on, one forgets. That's my greatest fear; I don't want to forget. I don't want to forget all the memories, the good times…or the bad. I feel if we forget any of that, David will truly be gone. I think it's our duty to remember; no matter how much it hurts."

—CAPTAIN CLINTON HALL, USMC—

"I was platoon commander in 2008 and it was around July when I first met David. You have to remember, I was an officer and he was enlisted. But I remember him as one of the quieter guys. To be honest with you, I can't recall any kind of first impression other than that." Captain Hall, who was still active duty at the time this interview took place, went further to say, "As an officer, I was a couple levels removed from being as familiar with Baker as the other guys were. But I can tell you this; God was important to him but not in an 'in-your-face' kind of way. His friends and the relationships he made along the way were important to him as well."

"When we were out doing our job, we had established six patrol positions. David was at the most northwest of them." Captain Hall paused. "I was only up there maybe 10-15% of the seven months we were there. But David, he was consistent. You knew what you were going to get out of him every time. He was always point man because everybody trusted him, trusted his common sense and his abilities to do all the things that the infantry trained him to do. As far as always being point," Hall paused a moment. "Baker always volunteered."

"You never had to worry about David being down in the dumps or depressed. He was a real positive guy. People would go to him, like the new-to-platoon guys. If they had any issues, they'd go to Baker, confident they wouldn't be turned away. And as far as attributes go, I'd say kindness and empathy;

attributes you wouldn't normally use to describe a 21-year old infantry Marine." Captain Hall spoke without hesitation.

I asked Captain Hall to describe a typical day for his Marines while they were in Afghanistan. "Typical day. There was no typical day. You didn't want typical because that meant routine and you didn't want routine, so there was nothing typical about any day." Hall voiced emphatically. "Times would constantly shift. That varied through the day and night patrols. Then there'd be some time spent on post, providing security for the rest of the guys. Maybe somewhere along the line, you'd have anywhere from four to eight hours of personal time for sleep and what not. But no patterns were established. We tried to avoid that."

"The day everything happened was absolutely not typical. There were around 160'ish Marines out that day all spread out across a mile. I was about 250 meters away from the unit David was with. He was point for his element, which is a stressful thing in and of itself but he was calm about it and was like, 'Nope. I got it. I'm the best guy for this' and he was."

"He was calibrating his metal detector when it happened. There was no reason to think there was an IED there; no indicators. That he and the other guys were able to stop all the other bad guys and their actions is a testament to their ability and will. They went into an unknown situation against a sneaky enemy and they never lost what they were at their core. They went, they returned home and they never sacrificed their ideals. I was never concerned with Baker or any of the other guys; they never lost who they were. I mean, after everything happened, they changed; we all did, but they stayed true at their cores."

When asked about memorials taking place while they were still in country, Hall responded, "When something like this happens, guys need to have some closure. So two or three days after Baker died, we had a memorial at COP Sullivan. It was the first roll call I had attended resulting from somebody trying to do us harm. Since we were still in country, obviously not everybody could attend. We had a full roll call at Camp Pendleton the following February."

"Immediately after everything happened, I was angry. It made me more determined we were going to accomplish the damn mission. "I grew frustrated when people'd ask if we were going to continue the mission. I was like 'If we don't, why did these guys die?"

"I spoke to his parents, and wrote them both letters. It was about three days following the death of Baker I contacted them on satellite phone."

"I certainly have not forgotten. I doubt I ever will. If anything, I train my officers even harder. I believe Baker lived the life he wanted. That event made me appreciate each day we have even more." Captain Hall fell silent in recollection.

—WILLIAM WHITLOCK, USMC—

"David and I served in the same platoon. We were good friends, but when it came time for deployment, I didn't go. I'd come to the 1/5 in 2008 and was put into their platoon when those guys were just getting back from deployment."

When asked to describe David, Whitlock used the following adjectives: "Fun, outgoing, funny guy (emphasis on really.)"

"David always lightened up a situation. Having him around was always good; he was always in a good mood. If you wanted to argue a point with him, or you brought something up, he'd call his mom and put her on speaker phone to prove a point. Every time we'd say something wrong, he'd call his mom and be like, 'I told you.'"

"Whenever anything bothered him, David didn't say much. You could tell he was in a mood; he wouldn't be upset or try to fight with anybody because of it. He was that kind of guy."

"I didn't go to Brannon. I wasn't able to go on that deployment. I was on the Wounded Warrior list. As a matter of fact, I get out next week on terminal leave. (Jan 2013). I've been in eight years."

"The things that meant most to Baker? His family and his friends. We were always hanging out with him and he always spoke highly of his family."

"I was at Camp Pendleton when David was KIA. Santoro was behind him when it happened. Baker's sister had called and asked about Santoro. Mama B. got 'the call' in-country. We only knew people had been hurt, no names were given.

So when we found out for sure, I was sick to my stomach. It seemed like everything stopped. I did go to Roll Call at Pendleton. It felt like there was this big shadow hanging over me. For me, that ceremony was sadder than hearing that it actually had happened. You see all the families that have to go through it. There've been others I've known."

"It's something like that makes you want to hold onto the friends you've got and not want to hold onto anything bad… because you never know."

"One story sticks out. David used to have his nipples pierced. We were all on our way to San Diego. ("German stayed sober that day," Whitlock laughed.) Me, David, and Simpson well, we all woke up with our nipples pierced. We had to go to Twenty-Nine Palms for deployment workshops so it was kind of funny I guess because we weren't supposed to have any piercings…"

"David was a good friend to have. He was just one of these guys you wanted as part of your group and have him around you everywhere'd you go."

—DAVID YENOWINE, FATHER OF KEVIN YENOWINE; USMC—

Mr. Yenowine's son Kevin was a Marine who served with Lcpl. Baker and was actually with him on patrol the day David was KIA. Mr. Yenowine was asked to contribute to David's biographical account because in addition to Baker's parents and family's views, the author felt sharing another parent's perspective on the events that happened that day in October 2009 might help others realize the scope and impact this event had.

"October of 2009 apparently was a hard month for Weapons Company as far as patrols went. My son was one of the Marines with David that day. Actually, David was Kevin's assistant gunner when they deployed to the Helmond Province."

"We got a call from Kevin in December and as soon as he spoke, I knew something was wrong. Kevin let us know he hadn't been seriously wounded and told us what happened. It was maybe several weeks later we received the letter he'd written telling us everything. I actually re-read that letter this morning; it was what happened through his eyes. This might put a different perspective to things."

"They'd been out on a patrol and had set up a perimeter to fly out some Afghan soldiers who'd been wounded earlier. Kevin had been walking toward some tree line, pushing through and spotted a compound (and walked up a small hill on the far side of landing zone for the ANA soldier medevac). The buildings were all empty from what he could see. Apparently, the Afghans vacate areas where they've placed IEDs so Kevin kind of stepped back and waited for his sergeant to tell them what to do next. David came up to clear the area with his metal detector and in the first swing was the IED. (Once the medevac had happened, they'd all congregated in the vicinity where Kevin had been posting security. They decided to sweep the graveyard so David began walking and the rest of them started following. The IED went off as he was pulling out his metal detector) Kevin was about 15 yards away. Apparently, moments before the explosion, the sergeant had leaned back to have Kevin adjust his radio. Then the explosion went off. Initially, Kevin thought he'd lost consciousness for a few seconds but as he later clarified, he wasn't actually knocked out. (As Kevin put it, "It had more to do with a memory lapse from either the blast or from being really freaked out.") When he got his wits back, Kevin thought he felt something on top of him. The staff sergeant and Santoro were closest so he thought it was one of them. Everybody jumped up and Kevin rolled over and saw David in the road. He'd originally thought the staff sergeant had lost an eye, not that it actually happened. Kevin had stopped a few steps before the blast because somebody had called his name.

"I believe it was hard for Kevin to maintain his military bearing after seeing that happen. David was his friend. Even after the blast, they still had a mission to complete. They all essentially got up, brushed themselves off and went on to check out those buildings."

"That particular day, David had taken point like he normally did on those kinds of missions. He liked to control the pace, protecting everybody. That day, that whole deployment definitely became life altering. That particular incident was a near miss for all those guys, my son included. After we found out what had happened, a couple things started going through my mind. We were glad Kevin was okay, but felt a little desperate, too because he was so far away. Until then, we'd never talked about combat. So that day, things started getting real. Besides, David wasn't the first loss that regiment experienced."

"I started doing a lot of thinking after that incident. You know, after you think about it, you're grateful your son is alive but you have to think about somebody else having lost their son. What do you do now? But that's the nature of it. There's a debt to be addressed. The family of the other guy? They're still there even though their loved one is not."

"The first thing I did was get on the Internet and find out about David. I left comments on a page and thought, 'Okay.' That was for now. But it didn't seem like enough. Time went on, anniversary dates rolled around..." Mr. Yenowine took an extended pause, deep in thought. "I work for a defense company. We had a Memorial Day event where employees could put up pictures. So I grabbed a picture of Kevin and David together, put David's name up, wrote a paragraph about what happened and posted it. That was one thing I did. Then the anniversary date came around and I sent a note of condolence to Baker's family. In it I told them about the remembrance wall at work, sending that off without expecting a response. Then in December of 2010, I went to Washington D.C. on business. 'Wreaths Across America' was there the same weekend so I managed to contact Laurie and asked if I could place a wreath on David's grave. She said sure, so I went to Arlington early and took some pictures, posting them immediately so she could see them. Somehow, that made me feel as if I were there for her, you know? I try to keep in touch." Mr. Yenowine's voice started to trail but he brightened immediately.

"Let me finish the story about the wreath. I was standing at David's grave the entire time after I had placed the wreath at his grave. There weren't any ornaments to it at all. I'd taken a picture to send and finished sending pictures to David's mom, never standing more than a few yards away from that wreath the entire time. I'd taken more pictures and realized while I was looking at them that there were ornaments on the wreath in the pictures. I mean..." Mr. Yenowine fell quiet. "—well, I don't know. I was there the entire time and those ornaments seemed to have suddenly appeared. I guess I was just intrigued by that."

"Kevin told me a little story about a night they were all out on patrol. They were moving along steady when the person in front of my son pulled ahead of the rest of the patrol. So they fell behind the person in front of them and soon found themselves on the other side of this small canal. 'How do we get across?' Kevin asked and Baker was like, '*Just jump.*' Apparently, because of their night vision, this canal didn't appear very wide (when in actuality, it was quite wide.) Kevin tried to get a little running start to jump it as best he could, but he landed in the water instead. So he started whispering loudly for help, (you know, they couldn't yell loud) and here comes Baker who'd apparently found a little foot bridge. He walked over, looked down at Kevin and said, '*My bad.*'

"I cannot begin to fathom what it's like for someone to lose a son in war. That's why I think we need to remember the price and acknowledge the debt. For all those guys who die doing their jobs in service to this country, I feel like the rest of us have been given a debt we're obligated to repay."

"Our son was interested in joining the military, period. My wife comes from a Navy family, but our son had already started talking to recruiters at school. He'd been doing the whole compare and contrast thing and chose to join the Marines. I wasn't sure he was going to get in but, well, he was the first to sign and three or four of his friends signed up as well."

"As a parent, I knew if my son was enlisting in the Marines, he was going to go to war. So I questioned the options, lined everything up to consider. I mean, we enabled him; and off he went. There's a lot of emotion to the Corps, and he wanted to be the best Marine he could be."

—KYLE SKEELS, USMC—

The interview with former Marine Kyle Skeels was both light-hearted and serious at the same time. It was obvious by the words he chose as he answered various interview questions presented to him that his life certainly was affected by the loss of his brother Marine Lcpl. Baker. Following the same list of questions presented to all of the other Marines and Navy veterans interviewed, the first question presented to Mr. Skeels asked about meeting David Baker for the first time.

Skeels laughed heartily before sharing his memories. "We met when I first got to the 1/5. It didn't take long to get in good with David. He was the guy who was always joking around. You know, new guys are usually quiet and scared but not David. He joked around all the time. He really lightened things up for everybody. When I first saw and heard him, I thought to myself, 'I gotta be friends with that guy.' And that's how it started."

"My first impression of David was—" Skeels paused in thought. "He was just a funny guy. He was the most unselfish person I have ever met in my life. He had so many good qualities but selflessness really stands out." Almost as an after-thought, Kyle added the following. "Probably the most outstanding thing about David would be his liveliness. I mean, I never saw somebody come off training, come back and go straight to Wal-Mart and get five bottles of Oakleaf Wine when everyone else was down. He'd get his wine then be up for hours drinking it." Kyle grew silent between questions. "Emotions on his sleeve? Let me say this; David was never afraid to tell you how he felt. He'd argue with you tooth and nail until you saw things his way. But even after the arguing, you wouldn't feel bitter. You'd feel happy after you were finished arguing a point with him, even if he won the argument."

"I'm sure everybody else has said this, but as far as things most important to David? That's easy. Family." Skeels spoke without any hesitation. "He was all about his family. That's all he wanted to was make his family happy. David would literally do anything to make his brother, sisters, and his parents happy."

"A day in Afghanistan; you'd wake up, well if you want to call it waking up. It was more like coming out of a daze that was like a nap if you were lucky. We did long hours of patrol, randomly, at any time. Things could go awry really fast. You had do what you had do to make it back alive. No matter what type of duty you were doing any particular day, you wanted to make sure all your guys were on their toes." Kyle paused as he thought of the next words he was going to share.

"The day we lost David was like any other day in Afghanistan. We knew we were going to be doing a raid that day, a really big one. I was on the radio at my post. I heard everything when it started going down. Matt (German) was on the radio. You could hear in his voice that something had happened. Eventually, everybody came back to base. When Matt came walking in, he was destroyed. All he said was, 'David' and I knew. I couldn't believe it. I was in shock, I couldn't believe what had happened." Skeels grew silent.

David's loss wasn't the only one the 1/5 would suffer on that deployment. There were several Memorial Roll Calls after everything happened; one in-country as well as one Stateside when the 1/5 returned. "I was at both ceremonies." Skeels revealed. "I did the placement of David's helmet. Honestly, it was one of the hardest things I've ever done in my life. I felt like it should have been, well, it just took so much out of you. You're standing there and looking over at the entire platoon, there's no way of getting away from all of the emotion."

"David was an amazing best friend, one I'll never have again. I wish I could have grown old knowing David all the way. I'm so proud to have known him. There's so many shitty people on this earth and then there was David. I was just honored to have had a friend like him." Kyle's voice softened as he shared his thoughts.

"You asked me to describe a particular event that stands out? There's so many, but I'll share this one. We were flying, a whole plane full of Marines. I think it was to Kurdistan or Afghanistan; I'm not sure which one. Everybody was nervous, completely silent getting onto this commercial plane. You could feel the tension. Everybody was quiet; except for one voice, which you heard above everything else. David. David asked the stewardess, '*What's for dinner? Chicken or chicken?*' It was absolutely hilarious."

"The world missed out on meeting one of the greatest people there has ever been. David signed up for the Marines knowing he could die, but it was for a purpose he believed in. He knew death was a possibility yet he enlisted anyway. He loved his family, friends and life. People like David have made this all possible, the way we are able to live today.

—JOHN CHENOWETH, USMC—

"I was David's recruiter. At the time, I was stationed in Mentor and had been recruiting for about six weeks. He was the second young man I enlisted into the Corps."

"About two weeks before starting recruiting, I'd been with the Marines stationed in Brook Park (a suburb of Cleveland). About twenty Marines from out there had been killed within the same day of each other so recruiting was very tough. That incident was at the forefront of everyone's minds. It was four months following that when David went up to enlist."

"I remember speaking with him for about three hours, then asking if he wanted to be a Marine. Without hesitation, he said yes and after that, he became a regular fixture at the office. He'd originally signed on to be an MP (military policeman) but didn't make all the quals (qualifications). By this time, his brother Mark had already enlisted and gone through Infantry. So David decided he wanted to go Infantry, too."

"Between March and October, he was coming by the office all the time. I was putting in long hours because as I mentioned, recruiting was very hard. Since I was in the office for such long hours, David would always ask if there was anything he could do for me. He'd do stuff like pick up a soda or something to take over to my wife (who worked across from my office) and small tasks like that. He eased the burden of my not being able to do those things." Chenoweth paused only briefly before answering the next question presented to him. "I'd have to call what Baker had a sense of selflessness. He was always thinking of others first."

"My first impression of David was of confident naiveté. He was one of those guys who was comfortable in his own skin. Looking back at it all, I'd also have to say he had an indestructible look in his eyes. It was like no matter what, he was going to tackle anything that came his way. Whatever it was going to be, he wasn't going to let it be a problem.

"When asked to further describe David, Cheno thought hard. "To break it down into words is just hard. I mean, I've already said 'selfless'. But David was thoughtful, too. He was caring, and he was a dependable young man."

"David's mom was emotional when another son left for boot camp. But when he came home, she saw a new man. David walked taller, stood straighter. He'd become a man in a period of about three months. So he came home, went back, hit SOI (which he was not happy with, by the way) and absolutely hated it. But halfway through, he was assigned to Mortar Platoon and he had a completely different attitude. That's when he was assigned to go to California."

"So fast-forward; I was no longer recruiting. I'd been off recruiting duty for barely over a year and was in Charleston, South Carolina flying. I was a navigator for C-130's. Since I had been off recruiting, I was out getting requalified and trained on everything. When I received news of David's death, we were doing drops and had ended up flying over the beach at about 2,000 feet. We hadn't been able to raise the ground guys on radios so everybody said, "Okay, let's use our cell phones." As we got to Myrtle Beach, my phone started vibrating. I'd forgotten to turn it off from earlier. The message was brief. 'D. Baker, Class of 2006 Riverside HS. LCpl KIA'. I literally crumbled into tears and frantically started texting everyone I could in Ohio. I got hold of Michael Hatton—" Cheno trailed off in silence.

"At that point, it'd been about 36 hours since David was killed. We'd landed and I just took off. I mean, still in my gear. I left my duties and hit the phone. Info was starting to slowly trickle in. I called Hatton and asked him to tell Laurie I was so very sorry and if she wanted to talk, I would hear whatever she had to say. He called me back and told me Laurie indeed wanted to speak to me. So later on, she called and was crying so hard. She asked me to be in Dover (Delaware) when David's body came in. I immediately called my wife, told her to meet me with my dress blues because we were meeting the plane in Dover. I literally ran from my plane and hit the car still in my flight suit. We made the three-and-a-half-hour trip to Dover in less than three hours, still missing David's arrival by about 30 minutes."

"We went to the hotel where the family was staying. We went up and my wife started talking to Little Mark as I changed into my dress blues. Mark came and took me up. Laurie immediately gave me a big hug and just started sobbing."

"The door opened and Big Mark walked through. 'Cheno, thank you so much for coming.' We talked for the next half hour or so and it was determined they wanted me to escort David from that point on. We began the escort process right then and there. No questions asked.

So I spent the night at Dover and went to receive instructions on what I was supposed to do. I went down there, secured extra flags for the family, because you know, ordinarily there's only one flag given but because of the circumstances..." Cheno paused once again. "They opened the casket to show me David. They had him completely covered, but it was my responsibility to make sure everything was just right. After completing everything at Dover, we flew to Cleveland. When we arrived, it was unbelievable. There were flags everywhere, motorcycles, police, fire fighters; all the way back to the funeral home. There wasn't an empty spot along the road. It was something you'd normally expect for dignitaries and such."

"We got David to the Funeral Home. I stayed the night with my pastor because the next day was calling hours. That all started at ten that morning. Laurie was having a breakdown. I know when the Ohio Senator showed up to offer condolences to Laurie and Big Mark, Laurie's father gave him a letter to deliver to President Obama which he promised to hand deliver.

At eight that night, the line at the funeral home still stretched out the door, around the corner; we had to make an announcement to get the crowds to move on because we had to clear out the funeral home by nine-thirty that evening.

"The next day, we gathered to take David back to the airport to fly to Washington and the same thing; every overpass on the Interstate had fire trucks displaying these huge flags and all along the streets there were just absolute throngs of people." Chenoweth's voice lowered as he continued. "We arrived in Washington. My folks, who live in DC met me and took me back to the house. My wife, who is a photographer, took numerous pictures of his funeral." Chenoweth paused again. "You know, somebody is always going to Arlington to make sure there's something at David's headstone."

"As far as Memorial Services go, I've been to several since David's. It rips my heart out every time." Cheno grew silent. "His death still affects my life today. In fact, David's death affected me for a longtime. I actually had to be told to end my grieving process and move on. David wouldn't have wanted me living life that way. It makes me think of that Bible verse,

'*Greater love has no one than this, than he who lay down his life for his friends...*" "He was an amazing young man. I'm saddened we were all cheated of the time we should have had."

Chenoweth made commentary inclusive of all the things that had happened following David's death. "We helped the family meet the Zac Brown Band ('*Chicken Fried*'). My wife told me they were going to be in Cleveland, so immediately, I began the process of establishing contact..." Chenoweth paused again. "And you know, for David's funeral, so many motorcycle groups showed up; even Hell's Angels. That was hilarious because you know, the cops don't usually take kindly to Hell's Angels. The general perception is that they show up to places with baseball bats and create trouble. They showed up with these huge Marine Corps flags, tightly rolled up. No ball bats that day."

"There was this one PGR (Patriot Guard Rider) guy at Arlington; their lead guy was this grey-haired, wiry-thin but muscular fellow. He had a POW/MIA flag on one side of his Harley and the American Flag on the other. It was great to see. They went with us all the way to Arlington. When David's funeral ended and we were all like, 'Now what?' I turned and looked over my shoulder. On one side was David's casket but on the other was the PGR, all standing in line; keeping watch and making sure nothing happened to David. The PGR doesn't get enough recognition."

—HEARD THE ONE ABOUT THE MUSICIAN, THE WRITER AND THE MARINE?—

"For God did not give us a spirit if timidity, but a spirit of power, of love and of self-discipline."
II Timothy 1:7

The ultimate inspiration and focus for this book was a Marine killed in action named David Raymond Baker. How this biography came into existence is a story unto itself, one complete with its own beginning, middle, and end. So many Marines, family and friends allowed the author opportunity to interview them for their stories about David that Fitzgerald figured she owed them all the story behind why she pursued being the one to write this book about David.

However, before the seeds were sown, more than a few individuals demanded: "Who the (insert your favorite expletives here) was this Fitzgerald person and who does he think he is to write a biography about Baker?" One could almost imagine the surprise as people found out Fitzgerald was in fact, a woman and a veteran to boot.

"I was NOT a fellow Marine; let me make that point perfectly clear. But as a fellow veteran, I felt I had a responsibility. Some people have started organizations, or organized charitable events to honor their fallen brothers.

The way I learned about this particular Marine (LCpl. Baker) was enough to instill in me a sense of responsibility, an obligation to do something for this country by way of honoring and remembering one of many Marines whose life was taken while in service to this country. I simply chose to write a book about a hero."

Everyone involved with this venture will recall the two-part statement conveyed to them at the beginning. As the author began the colossal task of completing the numerous phone calls, interviews, and collecting of information, she stated the project she was hoping to create about LCpl. Baker was not so much just another book she was writing as it was a compilation of other people's details and reminiscences that she wanted to weave together to honor the memory of a fallen Marine. The whole idea was to introduce the rest of the world to this specific Marine. After people read about David Baker, Fitzgerald wanted his name to be the one impressed upon their minds. However, despite all the explanation of plans and follow-up etc., there still seemed to be much hesitation and apprehension exhibited by numerous people in contacting and talking to the author. As a veteran herself, the author understood the underlying reasons behind why some chose not to allow her the favor of an interview. Because of that, she quickly determined it necessary to incorporate the following explanation.

From Yellow Ribbons to a Gold Star isn't a story derived from some superfluous faux news or gossip magazine. It wasn't snagged from some meaningless blog floating around on the Internet. Instead, this book became a compilation of stories and personal experiences shared about a man who was taken from this world too soon. It was an attempt to convey to the rest of the world the story of a kind, generous and fun-loving soul. These stories were about what and who he loved, who he was and still is to so many. Attempting to write the story of David Baker's life without specifically listing any other names would have been like challenging somebody to cross a raging river without a boat or bridge. The wonderment and admiration for anybody accomplishing such a feat wouldn't mean too much or be nearly as interesting without hearing the stories and adventures that were had along the way.

Why such a book? Why Fitzgerald? More than one person asked those questions through the lengthy process of conducting interviews. *"I always thought one of us would be the one to sit down and write a story about Baker"* voiced one OEF Marine. Why such a book? Because it's necessary. It's needed. Why Fitzgerald? Because nobody else had done it yet. And remember 'back story?' *'Put it where it's needed.'* People wondered how Fitzgerald happened to choose David as the Marine she wanted to write about. This next story explains it all.

Fitzgerald once had an unconventional, albeit first-rate friend named DJ Simon. Mr. Simon was an older gentleman, a dot-com, corporate kind of guy who, despite making his fortunes early in the computer industry, was still looking for that inspirational 'something' to fulfill his life. (http://www.davidjsimon.com) Simon was a man with adult children who was, incidentally also one of those people with the unfortunate designation of being a father who'd experienced the death of a child. Surviving several other heavy adversities in his own life, Simon made his mark in the computer industry early on without ever completely letting go of his musical aspirations.

Mr. Simon was an ambitious man, as well. In pursuit of his long-rested dream, Simon left Corporate America and soon saw his musical vision become reality, successfully recording a winning CD and touring the country doing what he loved to do best; play music. Meanwhile, at the same time about four hundred miles away, author Fitzgerald had been working diligently to capture a dream of her own. After putting the crowning touches on a story that had been three years in the making, the moment had finally arrived for Fitzgerald to quit deliberating and try publishing her story. However, in re-working a few of the final details, Fitzgerald found herself needing to research a collection of some overly familiar material.

Several more weeks passed before Fitzgerald forced herself to search out that last bit of material, some of which concerned the reasonably stock understanding how everybody only gets one chance to go through life so they'd better make the most of it the first time around. Fitzgerald was certain she'd heard that particular phrase somewhere and wanted to properly attribute it to its rightful owner. So she searched until she eventually found the answer. A musician living in Indiana (David J. Simon) had written a song entitled, Once Is Enough featuring the lyrics, *"You only get to go around once in this life, but if you do it right, once is enough."* One thing led to another and Fitzgerald eventually found contact information for Simon. To make a long story short, that was how she befriended musician DJ Simon.

Their friendship developed steadily over the course of the next several months as Simon would send samples of his music to Fitzgerald to listen to or she'd send him excerpts from her book to critique. It wasn't often they'd let any length of time pass between them without one of them leaving a friendly message for the other to read. During those early chats, Fitzgerald would prattle along about venues Simon might consider booking gigs after his CD was released, having no idea the caliber of musician Simon already was.

Fitzgerald was still on the fence about her book proposal that fall when she chanced to ask Simon if he'd consider being a test reader. "Bleed all over the pages. Tear it apart." Simon's first response was, "I'm no kind of reader" but before the end of the conversation, he'd accepted the challenge. Despite his initial proclamation, it only took Simon a short time to read through the manuscript.

"I might be dating myself here, but you know who Kurt Vonnegut is, right?" Invariably, they began discussing Slaughterhouse Five. Simon exclaimed, "You need to pursue your book. It's good," He chuckled heartily, "I'll definitely buy the first copy if you promise to come up here and autograph it for me." Simon's rave review was enough to encourage Fitzgerald to submit the manuscript. By the following May, she was notified it had been accepted and was consequently published. True to his word, Simon bought one of the first copies, posting notice of the fact for the entire world to read along with an artfully arranged photograph on the social network he and Fitzgerald shared.

"Stayed up way too late last night reading a fantastic book; couldn't put it down…had me in tears."

As a newly published author, Fitzgerald was given opportunity to purchase special hardcover editions. She immediately placed an order, intending to give those special editions as gifts of thanks to the various people who had taken on the challenge of test-reading and evaluating her manuscript. The first was ear-marked for Simon.

After his initial post and a flurry of message exchanges, Simon and Fitzgerald did not touch base with one another for several weeks. She knew he was busy promoting his CD and she was starting her own PR campaign for her book. At that time, Simon's musical success saw him traveling all across the northwest so she wasn't quite sure where to mail his gift. Fitzgerald waited as long as she could stand before finally checking in with Simon to see where he wanted her to send his autographed copy of her book. As she signed onto his social page, Fitzgerald noticed immediately something was amiss. It wasn't instantly clear as to what exactly but something had happened to her musician friend. With a slow-building dread, she began scrolling through numerous posts others had already left on his page. It only took a moment for Fitzgerald to discover her friend had not been in especially good health. The musical DJ Simon had unexpectedly died, alone at his cabin retreat in Idaho.

One night, several weeks after Simon's death, Fitzgerald sat reading through posts on her friend's web page for what she intended to be the last time. Around eight o'clock that evening, she received an innocuous pop-up message from somebody named Laurie. The message was simple and to the point. "How do I go about buying one of your books?" Fitzgerald glanced at the profile photo posted atop of the page, noting a handsome, young, Marine and automatically assumed Ms. Laurie to be his girlfriend. But Fitzgerald quickly learned how specifically Laurie was connected to the young man; the photo was her son David, a Marine recently killed in Afghanistan during Operation Enduring Freedom (OEF). The same month Fitzgerald lost her musician friend DJ Simon, another David materialized in her life; Lance Corporal David R. Baker, USMC. At the time, Fitzgerald wasn't sure how the turn of all those events fit together but figured there had to be a reason why Laurie's request showed up when and where it did.

When Fitzgerald initially started writing that first novel, her motivation was not to make fistfuls of money from it so much as to simply make a difference, to have an effect on just one life by words from her pen. The encouragement from her musician friend went a long way, but it would be because of a young Marine's mother that Fitzgerald would soon learn just how affecting her first book would become.

After Simon, Laurie bought one of the next soft-cover editions of Fitzgerald's novel, later revealing how she'd read it in its' entirety through the course of one evening. Fitzgerald later determined that had she changed the key characters, a few circumstances and key event around, the book could well have been written about Laurie's son. Fitzgerald and Baker's mother began corresponding quite frequently via the same social network her musician friend DJ Simon and she had utilized. Fitzgerald began learning about Laurie (Mama B.) and her family and was given to learn just how deeply sorrow had overtaken Laurie's life after her son was killed. While Fitzgerald found herself concerned each night with getting her own child off to bed, tucked in safe and sound, Laurie (or 'Mama B' as she was known) was enduring the loss of her youngest son to the war on terrorism. It didn't take a Marine to be affected by that.

Many a night after learning the complete story of this young man, Fitzgerald found herself scrolling regularly through the numerous articles and videos that had been posted across the Internet about him following his death. Baker wasn't just another guy in the military or some faceless casualty of war. He was a United States Marine named David Raymond Baker. He lacked only days from being three weeks shy of his twenty-second birthday, literally weeks away from completing his combat tour when he was killed by a pressure plate IED (improvised explosive device). More to the fact, LCpl. Baker was murdered in Afghanistan.

Three months after Baker's mother and Fitzgerald made their initial contact over the Internet, Fitzgerald had the unexpected opportunity to venture to Ohio to meet Mama B. and the rest of David's family. It was completely by Fate that Fitzgerald learned Mama B's other children (themselves grown adults) had arranged for a presentation of a flag in David's memory from Honor and Remember (a grassroots organization whose mission was to bestow such flags to every military family who'd lost a loved one in the perils of any war.)

Fitzgerald was already familiar with the organization because of research carried out for a previous project. She was quickly able to establish contact with the state of Ohio Honor and Remember representative and by sheer coincidence learned the weekend following Thanksgiving, a surprise ceremony was being held to honor Laurie's son at his Alma Mater, in Painesville, Ohio. After contacting Baker's family members for approval, Fitzgerald changed previous travel plans she had made for Oklahoma City and instead made the thirteen-hour drive north to attend David's ceremony in Ohio.

Mama B. and Fitzgerald briefly made contact with each another early the following Saturday via e-mail. Mama B. candidly revealed how her children had planned a surprise and that she was getting ready to go out with them for the afternoon. She casually asked Fitzgerald what she was up to for the weekend and the author nonchalantly revealed she and her family were headed to Riverside Drive in Memphis. (Mama B. had no idea Fitzgerald and her family had already made the trek to Ohio and were in fact checked in at a hotel, not far from her home.)

"You know, Riverside's the name of the road David's Alma Mater is on. All my kids went to school there. How funny is that?" It was all Fitzgerald could do not to reveal to Laurie that she was in Ohio that very moment, that it was her Riverside Drive she was going to.

Later that afternoon, a number of people began congregating in front of Riverside High School at a tree previously planted in David's memory. Shortly after Fitzgerald and her family arrived at the school, a number of local Leathernecks (motorcycle club) pulled in, as well as a variety of friends and family, and of course, the Ohio representative for Honor and Remember, Mr. Tom Mitchell. Fitzgerald had spoken at length with Mitchell a few days prior to the gathering, explaining how she had become acquainted with David's mother and asked if she might say a few words before he began his presentation. He graciously agreed.

Once Fitzgerald was sure everyone who was coming had arrived, she stepped forward to introduce herself. At this point she and Laurie (Mama B.) had yet to meet face to face, and although Laurie's children knew Fitzgerald had made it to town, their mother had no idea she was there, much less know she, herself was about to be presented an Honor and Remember flag.

As Fitzgerald introduced herself to those gathered out front of the school, an intense, petite, woman in a white, hooded sweatshirt burst from the small crowd assembled there and tearfully leaped forward. That was the first time the two women met, marking the beginning of a continuing friendship.

Later that day after the presentation, Fitzgerald and her family were invited to Laurie's home to visit at length with she and the rest of David's immediate family. During the course of conversation that flowed into the evening, Mama B.

humbly shared an uninterrupted treasure of various stories and information about David, proudly showing off his uniform which was prominently displayed in a shadow-box hanging in the living room. A brilliant red and gold Marine flag, presented by the Leather Neck Motorcycle Club—also encased, hung on an adjacent wall, signed by numerous Marines. (David's brother (and fellow Marine) Mark had taken this flag to Camp Pendleton for Marines of the 1/5, David's platoon to sign.) In the far corner sat a glass curio cabinet containing various mementos of Baker's life, items lending positive affirmation to the existence of their Marine.

Mama B. spoke with great fondness and affection, scarcely taking pause as she chronicled stories about her youngest son with the Fitzgeralds. The emotion and sincerity with which she conveyed those memories emphasized the fact she was still a profoundly grieving parent. David was clearly never far from her mind. Listening carefully to Mama B. as she shared her son's life, Fitzgerald automatically began taking mental notes.

Fighting the urge to let tears fall; Mama B. leaned forward conspiratorially and made her concluding remark.

"After everything happened, I've looked in so many places for something to help me understand all of this. But there isn't anything out there telling me how to deal with how I'm feeling; at least nothing that I've found. I mean, who expects this shit to happen to them?"

As the evening and conversation progressed, Fitzgerald matter-of-factly expressed her observations, and pointedly asked Mama B. if she realized how in a relatively short period of time, she had easily shared more than a few chapter's worth of information about her youngest son with virtual strangers? Eventually, the remark was made to Mama B. that she might consider starting a journal; create something tangible, concrete to document her feelings and experiences in as a grieving parent. Hesitant to say anything about it at first, (and not wanting to interrupt Mama B.) Fitzgerald looked around the table before she spoke again. "This is exactly why people write; because of stories like this. Think of all the mother's, parents, and families in your position you could help? Think of all the other parents who've been out there, who've looked for but never found that something to help them deal with their own loss?" Fitzgerald sat back in silence. She wasn't sure if any of that was the right thing to say, or the right moment in which to say it, but her words were already out there.

It seemed everybody stopped talking at once, holding their breath in anticipation as they waited for Laurie's reply. She leaned back slowly in her chair, studying Fitzgerald's face warily as eldest son Mark spoke from the kitchen counter.

"Ma, you could write a private journal. You wouldn't have to publish it. You wouldn't even have to let anybody read it if you didn't want. Just write things down. You could even burn it later if you wanted to, you know, if it helped—" David's brother let the comment trail as he quickly turned his attention back to his project cooking at the stove.

Mama B. sat back in silence. Pushing herself away from the table, she abruptly stood. "I need a cigarette." At that point in time, it was obvious she wasn't ready to seriously consider any idea about journaling, much less use her own grief to write a book.

It was getting late and the Fitzgeralds geared up to head back to their hotel. Mama B. had gone out ahead of them and was waiting to walk the family to their vehicle. Taking a final drag from her cigarette, she grasped T-M's hand and pressed a heavy coin into her palm. "David's unit was the first to have one of these issued to it. I want you to have this one." Fitzgerald looked at the challenge coin in her hand, immediately understanding the significance of the gesture.

Less than a year following the Honor and Remember flag presentation, Fitzgerald once again returned to Northeastern Ohio for an opportunity to attend and speak at an annual Veteran's Memorial service event. While she was in town, Mama B. invited her to stay with her and the family. Several months prior to the memorial, Fitzgerald had once more mentioned the idea of putting together a book. Sensing Mama B. still not receptive to the idea, Fitzgerald took a chance and proposed to the entire family that instead of material from their mother's point of view, how about putting together a biography about David?

Though a veteran herself, Fitzgerald was never presented opportunity to see or be deployed to another country in the line of duty. By the age of 21, Baker was already more worldly than she would ever be given to be. How was it she felt so capable of pulling together this particular Marine's biography? It stemmed from a sense of responsibility and obligation to Lance Corporal. Baker, his family, friends, and the world.

People do different things to remember the fallen. Some have organized and established annual events, such as footraces or poker-runs while others have held barbecues or special rallies for troops in general. Up to this point in time, nobody had yet sought to chronicle this Marine's life. After hearing the many stories and situations inclusive of David

Baker, Fitzgerald thought that people who would never meet, never know him, should be affected by his story. Just like the hundreds before and the hundreds after him, this Marine's was a story needing to be told.

In a letter to the family earlier that summer, T-M had written, "I'd be pleased if you'd all allow me the honor of writing David's biography." Mama B. immediately expressed to Fitzgerald that although she, herself would love to see such a book written, permission to compile the biography was a venture the entire family would ultimately have to agree upon. The first weekend in October 2012, just a few days after Baker's 25th birthday, it happened. The biography project was determined an admirable idea and the entire family allowed Fitzgerald to begin interviews immediately. *From Yellow Ribbons to a Gold Star* had become reality.

At the end of that same weekend as she was packing to return home, Fitzgerald chanced to ask David's brother Mark why he had decided to allow her to write his brother's story. Shrugging his lean shoulders, Mark looked at her with a sheepish grin and responded.

> *"I don't know. I've heard you speak. And everything you've said you were going to do for us, you've done. You came up here last year at the last minute for the Honor and Remember thing. I heard you speak then, and you came up here for this,"* He trailed off, a little uncomfortable with being put on the spot. *"—so why wouldn't I?"*

As Fitzgerald set about the task of contacting the numerous Marines and Naval Corpsmen who had served with David, it was brought to her attention on more than one occasion that, *"I thought when we got out and settled down that one of us would be the one to sit down and try writing a story about Baker."* Many who knew Baker expressed concern the author would want to delve too deep into details regarding circumstances surrounding David's death. So while initially many individuals favorably acknowledged their approval or vocalized support for the idea of a biography about their brother, there was still an air of hesitation and uncertainty; of suspicion. *"Explain to me again why you want to write a story about Baker?"* eventually gave way to *"What do you want to know?"*

How her first book found its way to the grieving mother of this particular fallen Marine remains a mystery, one not even Mama B. or Fitzgerald can figure out. Perhaps the most unusual details in all this explanation is the fact Fitzgerald was never blessed with meeting either of the amazing men ultimately responsible for the development of this book, never physically looked upon either of their faces; save for photos on one infamous social-network.

It was the concern of this Marine's family that their David (and all the other boys) never be forgotten;

> *"Arlington has all those headstones lined up in such perfect rows in every direction as far as your eyes can see. Then there are all the others you don't see, ones spread all over this country, other countries. All those white stones; they don't just represent fallen heroes. Those headstones represent so many broken hearts left behind; mother's hearts. So many cold, broken hearts…"*

Peculiar as it may sound, it was because of the first book Fitzgerald published as to how one surprise friendship led to another. It was for two men named David; one a musician and the other a young Marine, who each unknowingly established a powerful existence in her life that Fitzgerald became so compelled, so determined to pull the Baker Biography Project together. It was indirectly because of 'David the Musician' Fitzgerald chanced to become educated about 'David the Marine.' For reasons she cannot fully explain, Fitzgerald felt obligated, to do everything she could to help ease the ache of one Marine's grieving family's heart and preserve the memory of another American hero taken from this world too soon. As for wanting to write this young Marine's biography, Fitzgerald was determined to document the influence this young man had made in so many lives and honor his life and memory. Every time she was asked why she felt she should be the one to do this for this particular Marine, Fitzgerald shrugged.

"I set out to accomplish a specific goal with my first book. It was my expectation to touch just one life; and I touched a life. I've set a specific goal to accomplish in writing this book, as well; to make a hero's story accessible, to tell the story of a man who cannot tell his own." Respectfully borrowing from the Beirut Marine's promise to their brothers killed in Beirut in the tragic 1983 attack of the Marine barracks, Fitzgerald finished her explanation with, "The first duty is to remember." [5] That should apply to all our Marines; past and present."

—NUMQUAM OBLIVISCAR—

"Be on your guard; stand firm in the faith; be men of courage; be strong."
I Corinthians 16:13

The final chapter of this Marine's life began in a land far from home. David Baker's death affected various people, but his (as well as all of our military's losses) should have affected everybody. His death was outside that preconceived notion of what we like to believe is the usual order of life. Children are supposed to outlive their parents, get married and have children of their own, maybe even earn a college degree or start their own business. Baker wasn't killed at the local 7-Eleven or outside the Mom and Pop Grocery in Suburbia. David was not killed in a horrible car-wreck, which from a statistical stand-point, young men of his age-group should be more concerned about. Instead, David's life was stolen from him. He was a United States Marine, another casualty in the War on Terrorism. Perhaps what made this Marine's death harder to accept was that it was so random, yet so planned. If it wasn't Baker, it undoubtedly would have been somebody else. And it had been; over and over again.

Hundreds of American servicemen have been killed by IED's of various sorts, throughout a country located thousands of miles away from home. War isn't supposed to be personal? It's hard not to take it as such knowing somebody woke up that day with a job that necessitated preparation to kill as many Americans as possible. The IED claiming Baker's life could have killed anybody. But it didn't. It killed the young Marine from Ohio.

The war did not stop when Baker's life was taken, perhaps a fact making the death of this Marine all the harder to accept. While the rest of the world ignored the nightly casualty accounts of Operation Enduring Freedom, the military still had its job to do. Baker's family and friends were subjected to that constant reminder regarding why their Marine was killed in the first place. Not that they had to be reminded of the fact he was gone, but rather, the media would not let them forget.

It sounds cliché, but the fact Baker died so others could live is not something up for examination. The people who knew him were left to wonder though; would this war have changed David as it had so many others? Mama B., Baker's mother commented how she observed how deployments seemed to have affected many of David's fellow Marines and Corpsmen so negatively. She was left to wonder how it might have changed David as she shared how she had already detected changes in his facial features after he'd been sent to war. But David's family would never be given to know how deeply the war had likely changed him.

It was with reluctance and hesitation this compilation was declared complete. It is a book that became more an elongated eulogy, honoring a Marine who chose to fight for this country, enlisting in the Marine Corps during a time of war in an infantry MOS (military occupational specialty which, as stated chapters ago, pretty much guaranteed deployment into an active war zone). David Raymond Baker might never have been known to so many, might never have made it to a biography, to his place in history, had he not died. But more the point, Baker was here, brought into this world at the exact moment he was in 1987 to be everywhere he needed to be. David Raymond Baker accomplished more in twenty-two years, nineteen days than many men will in an entire lifetime.

>*"Every Marine who has ever lived is living still, in the Marines who claim the title today. It is that sense of belonging to something that will outlive your own mortality, which gives people a light to live by and a flame to mark their passing."* [18]

This book was meant to be a testament to who Lance Corporal David Raymond Baker was, and still is to so many. Aside from being a profoundly missed son, brother, grandson and friend, Baker had also become a part of something legendary. Baker was a United States Marine; a man who served with his brothers in combat, serving with men who formed unbreakable bonds under fire on foreign soil, defending their country. The Marines were part of his family, who, even after death, whose bonds would remain unbroken. Remember the statement 'Heartbroken mothers and teary-eyed Marines rank right up there as two of the saddest, most affecting visuals a person will ever see.'? Baker was their family, too; a brother called Marine. They haven't let go, either. Not for the first time, "Leave no man behind" became a poignant and meaningful statement to more than a handful of Marines the afternoon of 20 October 2009. A life doesn't have to be star-studded or action-packed to be significant. A life simply has to 'be'. David Baker was...and is still.

November 10, 2011

—WAR WASN'T ONLY THEIR HELL TO ENDURE—

"Blessed be the Lord my strength, which teacheth my hands to war, and my fingers to fight. My goodness and my fortune, my high tower and my deliverance, my shield, and he in whom I trust..."

Psalm 144:1-2

'*Heartbroken mothers and misty-eyed Marines rank right up there as two of the saddest, most emotionally moving images any person may ever chance to see.*'

—Unknown—

This isn't the first book written about anybody killed in a war, in Afghanistan, or even about a Marine. Everybody thinks they know who the Marines are[9] and right now, readers may be asking themselves, "Aren't there already enough books written about them?" Sure, there are countless books encompassing everything you'd ever want to know about the Corps from the branch's inception at that famed tavern, the constant wrangle between grunts (combat Marines) and pogs (people other than grunts), right down to modern day sequestration and how it has affected day to day operations.

From Yellow Ribbons to a Gold Star, the Biography of a Hero is the seemingly yet to be defined genre of book that could be written in remembrance for every man who has sacrificed/has fallen in the name of service to their country. This book, however is an account of one of many such men; a young Marine denied the right to his life, inarguably, a man who made everlasting impressions on the numerous lives he so briefly touched. It is not some imaginative story creatively generated to get a point across nor was it some random propaganda related work of fiction. This is a story told by many, but only about one; a brother to them all. This book was the story about a man who actually lived but was not given the opportunity to grow old. This Marine's name? Lance Corporal David Raymond Baker.

In addition to an extensive preamble by the author, a myriad of memories, thoughts, and occasions have been assembled in this collaboration not only to pay tribute to a fallen comrade and honor his memory but also to introduce him to the rest of the world. There are no appended photographs or copies of maps of any of the locations described in this book. There was no need; they were there, and by 'they', this means the people who were involved with this book and in David Baker's life. (Besides, this isn't a book about geography.)

Among these pages, along with the numerous and wide-ranging accounts regarding this fallen hero's life, readers found a story from the more personal side of war; the story of a little boy from Ohio who grew up and became a United States Marine. David Baker's tale is a variety of remarks, comments and accounts assembled from the memories and personal stories of various sources/individuals from all across the nation (quite literally from California to the New York Island.) The family, friends, and variety of other acquaintances of this Marine elected to share their memories and contribute to what began as simply 'The Baker Biography Project', circulating their memories about a man, a brother, and friend who no longer stood among them.

With still noticeable aches in their hearts, dozens of individuals shared memories of a man unable to chase the same dreams, goals and aspirations that they were permitted opportunity to pursue. (Keep in mind, the majority of those interviewed were men who went to war shortly after graduating high school.) Graciously, they shared select moments from their lives; moments that at this point in time seemed had been lived a lifetime ago. Quite expectedly, the process turned sensitive and emotional on more than one occasion, particularly for Baker's fellow Marines, as it was no easy track for those men to allow themselves to be interviewed about a period in their lives that was so life-affecting.

All people interviewed herein were going on with the routine business of living their lives. The majority of Marines and Corpsmen interviewed were attending college, getting married, starting families and settling into jobs and careers following their enlistment in the military. (Several were still active duty at the time of this book's inception.) Though the majority were working on settling into existence after serving their country, everybody interviewed shared something else in common. They were all moving on, but with one mutual element missing. Whether he was a friend, a family member, fellow Marine or combination of all the above, that common element was David Baker. He wasn't given opportunity to continue experiencing the events and occasions in his life such as those his friends and family were.

More a celebration of his existence, *From Yellow Ribbons to a Gold Star* is neither meant to be a categorical, all-encompassing, 'A to Z' account of David Baker's life nor an explicit narrative of the tragic circumstances surrounding the event unexpectedly claiming it. (The men who bore witness to the events of that day remember the details all too well.) This book was never intended to be a dark place so if you're looking for that kind of read, know it's not going to be such. This compilation of firsthand accounts and recollections gives regard to an upstanding young man who died in the line of duty.

David Baker touched many lives. It stands to reason why there are many sides to his story. If nothing else, this assortment of remembrances more than validates the kind of man he was and still is. Of course, unlike biographies written about many military heroes today, notably absent from this particular one are any spur-of-the-moment, off-the-cuff remarks made by Baker himself.

There are usually two sides to every story, but unfortunately, in Baker's case, there is only one; not his. Absent are any firsthand impressions or colorfully spontaneous comments people may have considered typical of Baker. There would be no specific questions answered by David himself regarding future aspirations or well-thought responses to inquiries regarding why he chose to become a Marine; no poignant moments of laughter or glistening eyes here; except in response to those questions answered by the people who knew him. That is why this biography should be considered a *compilation* as opposed to simply a story written by some third-party. The only task for the author here was to gather together the memories, moments, and impressions Baker left behind, and craft them into a single, cohesive collection.

As with service members in any other branch of the military, when a combat Marine is killed an action, (KIA) there soon forms an enormous pool of remembrance and recollection to draw from. Before beginning the intimidating (and at times overwhelming) process of contacting people for this extraordinary venture, author Fitzgerald was cautiously made aware that even though months and years had come to pass since Baker's life was taken, his brothers, family and friends all were and still remained tremendously protective of him; faithful to the man, the son, the friend, to the brother and fellow Marine.

With the launch of this biographical project, it was made clear to the author by various sources she'd better know what she was doing in compiling this Marine's biography. Not all requests for interviews and information were met positively. As a matter of fact, one of the first individuals approached for this project had no qualms in immediately shutting her down with a terse "No thank you" regarding the request for an interview. (Several other men who served with Baker declined speaking at all, and for them, Fitzgerald rested no reproach nor questioned their decision.) She realized full well what it was she was doing when making her inquiries; asking people and combat Marines to trust an unfamiliar, unknown person, an absolute stranger, to talk with and share their personal memories of a man, their brother and friend who was killed doing the same thing they were; defending this country. In effect, she was asking them to acknowledge their own immortality with each question she presented. As a matter of fact, Fitzgerald was advised to proceed with extreme care before several of the interviews for the fact events regarding Baker's death were still deeply effecting. (One Marine actually turned the tables and briefly interviewed her before choosing to elaborate about Baker.)

From the literally battle-scarred exteriors of his brother's souls, Fitzgerald slowly and thoughtfully proceeded through the course of interviewing this group of Marines and Corpsmen. Eventually, several of the more reluctant individuals unexpectedly decided to speak and when all was said and done, the final result was a collection of stories and memories shared by the people who lived by and knew David Baker best; his family, friends and fellow Marines. The challenge wasn't to tell the story about Baker as much as it was to share the one because of him.

Not surprisingly, each of these men's accounts proved to confirm the deeply-rooted bonds of Marine brotherhood. In addition to providing answers to the sometimes difficult questions asked of them, these brothers-in-arms on more than one occasion chose to share details about the private life of their brother as well, declaring how in the field, "Sometimes we knew more about each other than even our own families knew." Though just because they knew things about Baker and had an abundance of stories to tell didn't necessarily mean they were going to share all of them with the rest of the world. There were many side stories revealed under the condition of 'off the record'. Despite that fact, one unspoken point all of these men understood glaringly well; if anybody 'from the outside looking in' was ever going to learn or write about someone they knew virtually nothing about, somebody had to be willing to tell the first story. (How else would the rest of the world know anything about their world?) "Am I my brother's keeper?" In the Marines, the answer to that question is a resounding, "YES!"

Fitzgerald was given quickly to realize how strong the ties that bind Marines and its family members together are, that not even death can weaken such bonds. Before attempting to interview any of Baker's Navy Corpsmen or fellow Marines in particular, the author already knew it would be no easy matter for any of her perspective contacts to return to memories of the events they experienced that day (and following 20 October 2009). Questions were asked and answers were given, but it wasn't an instantaneous process. These OEF (Operation Enduring Freedom) Marines all fought the same war, were witness to the same events, but answers Fitzgerald received to her specific list of questions came from all different perspectives. (Many Marines maintained a not-so-subtle tendency in utilizing some exceptionally colorful metaphors with expert proficiency.) Accordingly, no two stories were alike; except when it came to memories of their fallen brother. As was pointed out several times, two people could have been standing right next to each other, been witness to the same thing but each person's memories of that moment were going to likely be recounted in totally different ways. Such discrepancies were not falsehoods or untruths on anybody's behalf. The experience of combat affects people in different ways and unless you've been there, that can be a difficult concept to grasp.

Despite the fact David Baker died outside the pre-conceived 'natural order' notion of life, he remains a significant presence in the lives of those fortunate enough to have ever known him. Although no longer walking among us, many would say Lance Corporal Baker led a rich and amazing life and in his wake left a palpable impact felt today. His was not an existence to have been completely eliminated by his passing but instead, Baker's existence became a presence, a driving force for many long after they begrudgingly accepted the reality of his death.

"We've got to do this; otherwise, all our brothers' deaths would have been in vain."

Anonymous OEF Marine

Shortly after beginning the interview process with his family, the author grew careful so as not to refer to Baker in the past tense. When it came to conducting those first interviews with family members in particular, it became obvious, very quickly that their Marine is (not was) still very much a part of their lives; every day.

"Does it bother me whether people talk about David in the past? The present? It used to, but not so much anymore. It's okay. They're just words, anyway. We know where he is, where he will always be." Baker's sister Lauren when asked how she acknowledged people speaking about her brother's life.

Fitzgerald, who was no stranger to the Marine Corps motto, "Semper Fidelis" was privileged to witness how fierce and close to their hearts many Marines take a cause. There's rock-solid rational behind all the recruiting slogans and campaigns people have seen and heard through the years; "There's no such thing as an ex-Marine." "The title is earned, never given." "You don't join the Marines, you become a Marine." Marines take their identity and character very seriously, in all aspects; just as the author took to the task of compiling Baker's biography. When Fitzgerald determined piecing together a project of this magnitude, of such importance, she recognized there'd be no room for error if only for sake of the fact Baker was (and still remains) a United States Marine; "One of the few, the proud." All other concerns quickly became secondary.

No matter who you are or from what walk of life you came, a recurring theme in all our lives is the fact everybody has a story to tell. This becomes a fact ringing particularly true when it comes to these (and any) combat Marines and their Corpsmen. Remember, this fact applies to all walks of life, even the people looking in from the outside. We all have a story to tell.

To combat veterans reading this; with regard to combat, do you remember ever being asked about civility when it came to war *("Civility: claiming and caring for one's identity, needs and beliefs without degrading someone else's in the process.")* [10] or rules of engagement (*"ROE dictate appropriate responses to actual or perceived threats faced by the armed forces of the United States."*) [12] Can anybody remember discussions when people asked what either of those things had to do with war or killing people? How about ever trying to explain what the Geneva Convention was to a civilian?

Remember talking to people when you first came back home, trying to answer questions casually tossed your way and some of the responses you received? Do you remember your reaction to them? Remember coming home on leave to all the pomp and circumstance and the difference when you came home for good?

Though not many will admit to it, Marines can be a sensitive lot; especially the older, wiser ones who have their wealth of life experiences behind them. (Maybe sensitive isn't the correct word; perhaps passionate or complex would be the better choice.) Despite occasions where a few well-meaning civilian souls inadvertently conceded their own ignorance when it came to things like deployment, tours of duty, or combat experience, those combat Marines likely (although perhaps begrudgingly) took pause and answered the questions they were asked. But many civilians weren't aware or understood why combat Marines (and their Corpsmen) appeared so sensitive or reluctant in obliging with answers. No matter who asked what question, a Marine likely won't be forgetful of those other moments in his life when he patiently tried answering a well-intentioned question but the listener never made it past the preamble. (Mention 'Geneva Convention' or try explaining to a civilian what a CAR (combat action ribbon) is and watch their eyes glaze over in real time.) Too often, the Marine simply turned and walked away thinking, "Why bother?"

People quickly lost interest at the first mention of civility or Rules of Engagement. Civilians don't understand (they can't understand) when they ask a combat veteran questions about deployment, it's neither easy nor simple for him to come up with a response on the spot. However, understanding is a two-way street. Whether they want to admit to it or not, it becomes the task of those who do know to educate (not condemn) those who don't. So about all those well-meaning civilians who on occasion innocently asked, "What was it like to fight over there? Did you ever have to kill anybody?" Don't be too hard on them for asking. There's no course any noncombatant can take instructing them on the topics he or she can or should ask a combat Vet. At least they're asking, and that's a start.

War doesn't seem to be a matter of concern for people uninvolved with it unless there's a good, action-packed story attached. Unfortunately, it's the days when all hell broke loose that the people 'back home' want to hear about the most. Therein lay but one part of a multifaceted problem. Because whether or not every day was an action-packed episode (and most combat veterans will tell you those were the days they prayed didn't happen), war was still war. Despite specific events being deeply ingrained in their minds and hearts, never to be forgotten, civilians need to know it's generally those kinds of days combat Marines (and their Navy Corpsmen) wish they could remember the least.

In the immortal words of the Rolling Stones, "*You can't always get what you want.*" So while everybody has their own, unique tale to tell, the country as a whole needs to specifically remember all the men who also had their stories but didn't get to come home to tell them; men who, no longer able to speak for themselves, came home under a flag instead of saluting one, men who became stories themselves. What about all of them? Those men still have stories, stories in serious need of being voiced but because of one circumstance or another, their stories were destined to have different endings and be communicated by somebody else. Stories about war need not be inclusive of violence and bloodshed to warrant being told. Stories about war need to be told, period.

Marines die doing what they're told to do, being where they're told to be. "People shooting at you, plotting against you, it's just a regular day in the life of a Marine." [9] That's just the fact. They don't question, they just go. In and after any given battle, operation or campaign, who knows precisely the number of lives affected? Taken? The precise number of men whose stories will never be heard? It's safe to assume there are hundreds; thousands, when to even say 'one' is one too many. Many people don't understand combat, much less the Geneva Convention or Rules of Engagement. War is war, right? Isn't it supposed to be all about 'kill or be killed'; 'Shoot first and ask questions later?' It's hard for non-combatants to fathom how so many Marines have died simply because of where they happened to be standing, walking, driving or even sleeping at a particular moment; dying for this country while never anticipating 'today will be the day.' It's called doing their job, and they do it 'there' (wherever 'there' may be) so we don't have to worry about doing it here. "You serve where you're assigned." [Ibid.]

There hasn't been a draft used in United States since 1973, [27] so every man (and woman) who has chosen to be a Marine since that time has done so on their own free will, as did all their friends. (That should make it easier for people to understand the mindset of a Marine—especially of a recruit who opts to enlist in an infantry position during an active time of war such as Baker did.) Marines die doing what they do so the people 'back home' may continue doing all the things they enjoy doing without fear of _____ (insert your choice of censorship or form of foreign government control here.) Barely out of high school, many new Marines enlist thinking their eyes are wide open and then seeing more than they bargained for. [9] *"Marines do what they are told—no complaints. Duty, honor, country...generations of tradition in that."* [Ibid.]

Although time has passed and the questions are now different, there's something new for combat veterans to consider; the next time any civilian who *"—doesn't have a fucking clue"* asks what it was like to fight 'over there', remember all those men, those brothers who cannot tell their own stories. Remember the legacies each of them left behind and instead of being so hard on the civilians, engage them. (Statistically, there are more of them than there are combat Marines, so patience is key.) Draw them in and make it hard to lose interest and walk away unaffected. Have him or her pull up a chair and start telling the story of a fallen brother; tell them the story about a Lance Corporal named David Baker.

"You've got to learn from your history. If you don't have that, you've got nothing. We celebrate the wrong heroes. They (Marines) gave all for this country. How can anybody forget that?"

(Ayres)

"Those who fail to heed the lessons of history are doomed to repeat them."

(George Santayana, Philosopher)

Concluding this compilation is a poem which may be familiar particularly if you are a veteran. The man attributed with inspiring David Baker to join the Marines talked about this poem during the interview session conducted for this book and decided to search for and submit the copy he read from to include in Baker's biography. Mike Hatton revealed, *"I haven't read over this since the day of David's funeral at Arlington."*

There has been much controversy over attribution of this poem. Supposedly unknown in accordance to some resources, written by somebody's grandfather here or somebody uncle over there. Yet another source states it was originally written during WWI. What follows is the version Hatton submitted.

One website had a collection of comments about this poem, especially the last verse. However, the author believed one man may have summed it up best when he commented, *"To be totally frank, they all went through hell, so, to be honest, it may not have just one writer. Sure, someone wrote it first, but each version reflects their experiences."* [26]

—GOD BLESS YOU MARINE—

Version by Hal Popplewell. USMC 1971-1979
(Contributed by Michael Hatton, USMC)

You can have your Army khakis
And your Navy blues,
Here's a different sort of fighting man,
I'll introduce to you.
His uniform is unlike
Any you've ever seen;
The Germans called him Devil Dog,
But his real name is Marine!
He was born on Parris Island
The land that God forgot.
The sand was 14 inches deep
And the sun was blazing hot.
He'd get up every morning,
Way before the sun,
And he'd run a hundred miles or more,
Before the day was done.
He fought in the cold of Korea,
And in the heat of Vietnam.
Whenever our country goes to war,
The Marines are first to land.
We'll fight them on the ground,
We'll fight them in the sky,
When Army and Navy are heading home,

The Marines are standing by.
And when he gets to heaven,
St. Peter he will tell,
"Another Marine reporting, Sir,
I've served my time in hell!"

—ACKNOWLEDGEMENTS AND THANKS—

In Afghanistan (or any other country one might find themself in during a time of conflict or war), a Marine may start the day off by thinking about how yesterday was one hell of a day, or breathe great sighs of relief as he wonders how he made it through sleeping one more night in the front seat of a Humvee. A Marine may rub the stubble on his chin or shake his head at the heat index of the day or have finally lost track of the number of days it's been since he's had a hot shower. Whatever his thoughts are, most assuredly, he never starts the day off speculating whether or not today is a going to be a good day to die, particularly when he is at or around the point in life when other men his age are graduating (or due to be) from college or getting married and starting families. But what if?

In the relatively short span of time it took for me to track down, contact, connect with and interview the numerous people I could access from David Baker's life, I learned a great deal about the caliber and strength of friendships this Marine forged.

It was not my intent to be politically correct, nor mistakenly believe I was going to please all people everywhere when it came down to the brass tacks of publishing this compilation. I saw a need, requested the honor, and assembled this biography to honor LCpl. David Raymond Baker. That was my mission.

Everybody else told the story. With the dozens of interviews completed, one thing became glaringly clear; there wouldn't be enough pages to tell every story every person wanted to articulate.

The effects of combat are far-reaching, long affecting. It must be remembered people present at the exact same moment, witnessing the same exact event will likely have different accounts of the incident to share. David still had his story to tell; it just ended up being told by those who knew him.

This book couldn't be all-encompassing like the biography of Chesty Puller or Bud Dey. It wasn't thorough or complete from top to bottom. *From Yellow Ribbons to a Gold Star; The Biography of a Hero: LCpl. David R. Baker* was written to give people who never knew this Marine a glimpse into a life taken too soon, to put a solid identity to just one of the thousands of statistics of war and ensure one less man would be forgotten. It wasn't meant to slight any other branch of the military. However, keep in mind this book is the account of one specific Marine; David Raymond Baker. And if in reading this somebody discovers particular names or statistics missing, that's probably because they are, and quite purposefully, too. As the person who compiled the stories creating the foundation for this book, I was accountable for all content. Given the fact so many were and still are so protective of this Marine, you may be assured every 'i' was dotted and every 'T' was crossed. The name on the front of this book is 'Baker'. This biography was written to do more than simply put a picture to the price of freedom.

Given the fact people were first made aware of the *Baker Biography Project* in the beginning of October of 2012, and multiple attempts were made with many individuals in seeking access for the interview process, if there are any specific accounts not noted here, it was not by oversight. It was a choice. Some individuals would not speak about topics related to David's biography and other arrangements were attempted to include those individuals' experiences. For others, it was a matter of Baker's death being too difficult a topic, a matter too close to their hearts, too close to home; still. I held (and continue to hold) tremendous respect for all the men who participated in this venture, actively or not.

Interviews appeared in no particular order other than perhaps how one account naturally led into another. There is no first, last or otherwise order. I wanted to express enormous gratitude to everyone who chose to participate in making this project a reality. Thank you to all the Marines, Devil Docs, family and friends who made this happen.

—SOMETIMES EVEN MARINES CRY—

T-M Fitzgerald
07/29/2012

Holding the last drag as long as he could, he finished his last cigarette and then abruptly excused himself…

Mysterious…yet so serious, only he could tell you why—
Too frequently left to his own devices, he swore, "I'll be damned if they'll ever see me cry."
Too often he'd startle awake at night, pulling obscure thoughts from midair—
"How would anyone find me?" he'd ask, Then stare blankly at the chair.
Some would kindly ask 'What's wrong?' Then dare comment— "You shouldn't dwell…"
They had no way of knowing why…Why his life had become such hell.
So he sat there lost within his thoughts, searching to the depths of his soul…
Debating his life for one more night, Wondering if his story would be told.
He thought of friends as lumps filled his throat—hot tears welled in his eyes…

The things he saw, didn't want to see, and had long since
learned to despise…

In vain he tried catching shooting stars, Wishing hard as they
tumbled from the sky…

He'd look down into his empty hands, And only then, thought
to ask, "Why?"

He worried very little 'bout dyin', and one day he locked the door…

Wasn't worried today, he'd made his decision; He wasn't
comin' back anymore.

The people in those glasshouses there? He wished they'd stop
throwin' stones…

And if nobody truly meant it when they 'offered a hand?'

Then he preferred they left him alone.

It'd all be over soon enough, If the fat lady would just shut up
and sing—

But each day, he'd wait and each day would retire… Without
hearing a solitary thing.

And the knife throwing guy? He saw him, too—In the shadows
over by the door…

The guy who's blind? He's a fake, too. He don't need to come
'round no more.

His journey began where others' had ended… Events well
beyond comprehension.

He couldn't believe, couldn't fathom the things—The factors
everyone had so failed to mention.

So he got sent back home, With more guilt than he'd known—

(And you know? That crazy bitch never did sing.)

He quit all his frettin' and began years of regrettin'…

His only satisfaction was knowing that he'd tried.

It was then…

And only then…

When that Marine took pause…

Stepped down from that chair…

And cried.

———

—ENDINGS—

"No man that warreth entangleth himself with the affairs of this life; that he may please him who hath chosen him to be a soldier."

2 Timothy 2:4

To what extent can a man be considered a hero? How does anybody answer that question?

With the undertaking of this biographical journey, I was given to acquaint with a variety of Marines and Navy Corpsman who each had seemingly the almost instinctual ability to take care of matters concerning a brother/fellow Marine David Baker. Despite their sometimes colorful vernacular (which was a given) and rough exteriors, these men (veterans of Operation Enduring Freedom (OEF)and Beirut era Marines/Corpsman) gave some of the most expressive interviews I have ever taken as they shared memories and experiences (both on and off the record) about their fallen brother. This Marine would have been honored to be thought of so reverently by his peers.

With acknowledging the death of anybody who has made such positive impacts on the lives of others, we also tend to inadvertently analyze our lives; the shortcomings, the fortunes, the natural progression of each event in the scheme of life. What we discover may not always make us proud. However, if nothing else, we usually find ourselves waking up in time to smell the roses.

On Memorial Day Weekend 2013, I stood among men whose job it was to defend this country, who knew before they even signed the line what the potential outcome could have been. I found myself wondering that day what they were thinking as I caught many reflective gazes, feeling almost intrusive as I witnessed similar scenes over and over again throughout Arlington. The defining moment of that place in time actually came when all was said and done as everybody readied to leave Section 60 and head for the gates. For one split second, I believe I was given to know what it felt like to lose a son, a brother, a family member. As I saw the expression on each face before me; one by one and then collectively, the depth of emotion I witnessed at Arlington illustrated the point this Marine would never be forgotten.

"Heroes are made by the paths they choose, not the powers they are graced with." [4]

Initially, the idea behind the book you are holding in your hands was to simply gather a collection of individual, firsthand accounts from the intriguing cast of family, friend's, fellow Marines and Corpsmen to honor the memory of a man whose footsteps were felled too soon on foreign soil. Instead, it evolved into something much more, turning into a compilation that by all rights should have been basis for this particular young Marine's own memoirs, an autobiography he might have deliberated writing for a future child's sake. But there would be no campaigns or battle scars or any remarkable, firsthand exploits to tell stories about here.

Instead of penning his own life story, *From Yellow Ribbons to a Gold Star, The Biography of a Hero. Lcpl David R. Baker, USMC* became a combination of obligation and promise made by an individual whom David Baker never met to assemble his story for him. There'd be no detailing impressive deeds occurring over a potentially illustrious military career nor are there are chapters accounting feats accomplished against overwhelming odds. (After all, is that not what the rest of the world expects a story about a Marine to be about?) It is what it is because this is how it was told.

This book leapt from humble beginnings; a collaboration initially known as '*The Baker Biography Project*,' this collection of eclectic musings and collaborated accounts turned into a biographical journey about a man whose life more than mattered to those he left behind. Before all was said and done, this compilation turned into a manual of not only the biography of one (of the many) face of freedom but also a book filled with many second thought asides; reflections brought to light from the hearts and minds of those who knew this man so well both as a civilian and a Marine.

"As long as somebody remembers, heroes never die."
—Unknown—

Hero: A *man of distinguished valor or enterprise in danger, or fortitude in suffering; a prominent or central personage in any remarkable action or event; hence, a great or illustrious person.* [31]

Heroes aren't made. They just are. A quote found on the Internet posted by a man known simply as 'Samson' stated the following; "The word HERO should only be reserved for guys who knew death was imminent, yet chose to act regardless…"

When nonmilitary persons see or use the word hero to talk about any members of our military, many assume the designation is reserved only for high profile members they've read about or may happened to have seen on television. (You know, those individuals who've beat insurmountable odds, performed or acted above and beyond their expected roles in the line of duty.) In many minds, images of military heroes invariably begin with thoughts of Delta Force, Green Berets, Army Rangers or Navy Seals. While that may appear how things generally go, it's certainly not always the case. While Special Forces have undoubtedly birthed their share of heroes, there's something more humble than that in how a hero can be defined. Every war has its own and they're not as hard to recognize as people may believe.

Though certainly a subjective term, the word 'hero' encompasses all those men who made the decision to become part of the greatest, currently all-volunteer military force that protects our country and its' interests from enemies foreign and domestic. What makes a hero truly a hero? It's not always just about the person; location often has everything to do with why particular people come to be touted as heroes. And occupation? Always.

Hero is not specific to any one person, action, or location. In fact, many men who found themselves designated as such weren't aware anybody considered them heroes. Some rise without regard from already disciplined ranks to endure additional training, time away from their families and the world they knew outside the military. They accept the possibility, the potential of finding themselves in danger, all in the name of protecting what so many back home take for granted; freedom. Joining the ranks of those who've fallen before them, many given the title never knew it was conferred upon them at all. But for those they leave behind? They remember. This book would not have been conceivable without that detail. "To be heroic does not have to mean possessing the ability to stand against the evils of the world, either well or successfully—but just that one is willing to stand." [2]

From *Yellow Ribbons to a Gold Star; the Biography of a Hero: LCpl. David R. Baker, USMC* would not have been possible without them; heroes AKA Devil Dogs and Docs (Marines, their Navy Corpsmen as well as all the other branches of the military.) Incredible thankfulness and gratitude go out to them all and each of this particular Marine's family and friends who elected to contribute to this exertion; every one of them who so generously shared their memories and moments with such honesty and lack of pretense. If nothing else, in reading this tale of LCpl. David Raymond Baker, one categorical truism will become blatantly clear: "A Marine is a Marine, always."

It is with tremendous respect and appreciation I list the names of those who chose to support this project. (I believe I kept accurate record of them all, but if I've failed to note any particular name, please forgive me and know it was not on purpose.) First and foremost, I extend infinite and profound gratitude to David Baker's family for allowing me the incredible honor and opportunity to pay respect to their Marine in this manner. I thank Baker's parents Mark Sr. and Laurie 'Mama B.' for bringing him into this world; David's older brother (and fellow Marine) Mark and wife Maxxine "So you're the one" Baker, (the sister-in-law David never met who also designed the original cover of this book), and David's twin sisters Taylor and Lauren for all agreeing to the idea of this biography. I appreciate having been so graciously invited into their home to conduct in-depth interviews and be exposed firsthand to precious memories of their Marine. Together they shared a myriad of letters/correspondence, and various videos and audio recordings; the treasured possessions and reminders of Lance Corporal David R. Baker.

It was no simple task for anybody to recall the specific moments I inquired about. There were some definite weighty moments encountered with all of the asking however, despite the deep emotion, and expected melancholy, there were also many occasions of laughter as well. The focus of this compilation wasn't meant to be downhearted, but to celebrate this Marine's life.

Also to be thanked are Ashley O. (the girl David left behind), Thomas Isabella, Marc Jacobs, Roland McNeil, (hometown friends) and Bill Wade (Baker's former high school chemistry teacher/baseball coach), who each so generously contributed stories regarding the distinctive friendship they each shared with David.

I extend appreciation also to Tom Mitchell, (Ohio representative for the Honor and Remember organization) for taking time to answer the various questions I presented.

"There's no such thing as an atheist in a foxhole. If somebody doesn't have a God, they'll borrow yours. You don't wanna wait 'til then, though."

T. Hill 2012

In an era where electronic progress and social media networks change seemingly by the hour, I extend special appreciation to Baker's mother Laurie aka 'Mama B.' for personally contacting the men (Baker's fellow Marines and their Navy Corpsmen) who served in The 1/5 with David and for encouraging them to contact me for interviews. Had this endeavor taken place twenty years ago, connecting with each of these men would've been a much more difficult task to assume. This biography would not have been completed so thoroughly or so quickly.

With continuing gratitude, I thank the following Marines and Navy personnel for sharing their experiences about the man this book is about and for all the thoughts, recommendations, and ideas many made along the way: Steve Aragon, Travis Armenta, Jimmy Beran, John 'Cheno' Chenoweth (David's recruiter), William Childs, Daniel 'Doc'

Clemons, Matthew Dean, Matthew German, Dan Guider, Cpt. Clinton Hall, Michael Hatton, Dennis Holmes, Micah 'Doc' James, Michael Jones-Ritter, Brian Monahan, Vincent Morales, Jamison O'Connell, Ian Plumlee, Staff Sergeant Nickomar Santana, (and wife Shannon), Scott Santoro, Trever Simpson, Kyle Skeels, Matthew Torres, William Whitlock, and Kevin Yenowine (and his father David). Speaking and working with each and every one of you was an honor that provided the solid foundation this epic obligation stood upon. Your accountability was tremendously appreciated.

I am likewise grateful to the assortment of individuals (inclusive of additional members of the military, of course) who contributed to this project under condition of anonymity; extending recognition and profound appreciation to each of you, as well as to the individuals who (for personal reasons or otherwise) could not/would not grant me interview opportunities for this project. You deserve recognition as well; your contributions are not forgotten.

I would be remiss if I failed to extend gratitude and recognition to another group of Marines (and their various associates) who, in the summer previous to the launch of this biographical account, (2012) inadvertently helped David Baker's story see the light of day. Although a generation (plus or minus five to ten years) separated the timing of events each group of Marines were involved in, the elder group of Devil Dogs lent a supportive (albeit unknowing) hand in the creation of LCpl. Baker's biography. I want to thank the small contingency of Beirut-era Marines (and their Navy Corpsman) who endured my presence among them and theirs the fine occasion I was first given to witness that famed Marine 'espirit de corps' firsthand. (Espirit de Corps: "The unifying spirit inspiring enthusiasm, devotion, and unswerving regard for the honor of the group, an intangible attribute, yet one strong enough to motivate fierce loyalty and heroic deeds.") [18]

Present in that group from that era of Marines were Kevin Ayres (and his companion Rebecca Hamilton), Jeff Dadich, William (Bill) and Mona Harrison (*both* USMC veterans), Jack McDonald, Ron Moore, Bryan Westrick (and wife Kelli), and Navy Corpsman Steve 'Doc' Sibille.

In pulling this collaboration together, I also had the fortune of consulting with and making numerous inquiries of a variety of other Marines and Navy Corpsmen across the nation. I thank the following for their dialogue and allowing my sometimes unwitting (but always well-meaning) inquiries and for inspiring boundless insight and brilliant discussions: Ernie Brown, Bill Kilgore, Gary Lewis, Matt Torres, and Dwayne 'Doc' Walters.

There were more than a few nights I found myself up past bedtime chatting with these individuals on one coast or the other (via phone or social network) gleaning supportive information for Baker's biography. Thank you gentlemen, for enabling me the opportunity to enhance the clarity of various topics introduced in this book and so meaningfully connecting one generation of Devil Dogs (and Docs) to another.

I express special thanks to David Baker's fellow Marines Matt German and Trever Simpson who, after David's family, proofed the rough manuscript, reviewing its content for accuracy and clarity before it was submitted for the final editing process. I also thank Mr. and Mrs. Nickomar Santana for taking the time to test read and critique this biography as well arranging for and escorting me onto Camps Lejeune, Geiger, and New River Air Base in Jacksonville, NC.

There's one critical point to bring to the attention of any non-Marine who may be reading this compilation. When mentioning Combat Marines, one must be careful to also make note of their Navy Corpsmen. Marines don't train Corpsmen specifically but the Marines are a department of the Navy and in a nutshell, it generally goes without saying that without one, there isn't the other. Anywhere there's a hurt Marine, his Doc is never far behind. In this book, I make specific effort to always mention the two together when expressing thanks or discussing either group. So know any failure to reference one designation alongside the other was in no way intended to disrespect. "Corpsman up!" (However, this was, after all, a book about a Marine named Baker.)

I convey my most solicitous and sincere gratitude to David Baker for voluntarily choosing to represent and defend this country; a young man who, by many persons speculations was college-bound and destined for a career in law enforcement but instead elected to become a United States Marine and ultimately paid the highest price any man could offer; selflessly doing his part to ensure the freedoms of millions of people he did not know. Sometimes, even though war is generally filled with life-defining moments, we forget the individuals who fight such battles and don't get to come home. This book was compiled to assure forgetting this Marine would not be an option.

—'CHICKEN FRIED'—

"I thank God for my life—
And for the stars and stripes…
May freedom forever fly—
Let it ring…
Salute the ones who died—
The ones that gave their lives—
So we don't have to sacrifice,
All the things we love…"

—Zac Brown Band

David Baker was one of those people whom some have described as having that 'it' factor. This book wasn't written because of how David was taken from this world. It's a book that probably would have been written anyway had he the luxury of growing old. Unfortunately, the time for his biography came sooner.

"Don't mourn the fact this Marine died, but instead remember and be glad that he lived."

"Fair winds and following seas, LCpl. Baker."
Semper Fidelis

APPENDIX

7-Ton—A type of truck used in the military. 7-ton refers to its payload.

AK's—Refers to the AK-47, an assault rifle.

AO—"Area of operation"—In the military, this is essentially where everybody goes to work everyday.

CAR—This is a decoration/ribbon awarded to those who have actively participated in actual combat on the ground during a time of war.

COP—"Combat Outpost" A military post located apart from the main base of operation.

Corpsman—United States Navy trained medical personnel usually imbedded with

United States Marines.

EOD-"Explosive Ordinance Disposal" Personnel trained in rendering explosives harmless.

Firefight—The exchange of gunfire between opposing forces.

FOB—"Forward Operating Base" A secured military position used to support military operations.

IED—"Improvised explosive device" A homemade bomb made and used in unconventional ways.

KIA—"Killed in Action"

LCpl—"Lance Corporal" Rank in the Marine Corps directly below Corporal.

MCRD—"Marine Corps Recruiting Depot"

BIBLIOGRAPHY

1. Amendariz-Clark, M. Pvt, USMC; "Quotes about Marines." 20 September 2001, p.1, New York Times. http://oldcorps.org/USMC/ quotes.html.

2. Alsford, Mike. Heroes and Villains. Baylor University Press, Waco, TX. 2006.

3. American Gold Star Mothers, Inc. www. goldstarmoms.com.

4. Ashton, Brodi. Everneath. Harper Collins, January 2012.

6. Binyon, Lawrence. "Ode of Remembrance" From: "For the Fallen". The Times, September, 1914.

7. Blue Jacket. "The United States Naval History and Graphics Site."www.bluejacket.com.

8. Butz, Michael C. "Fallen Marines Home: Body of Painesville Twp. Man Killed in Afghanistan Arrives Friday, October 30, 2009."http://www.news-herald.com/articles/2009/10/30/news/nh1630888.prt.

9. Coram, Robert. "American Patriot: The Life and Wars of Colonel Bud Day."03 May 2007. Little, Brown & Company.

10. Dahnke, Cassandra and Spath, Tomas. Institute for Civility in Government. http://www .institute for civil-ity.org/who-we-are/what-is-civility.aspx.

11. Doyle, Clive with Wessinger, Catherine and Wittmer, Matthew." A Journey to Waco: Autobiography of a Branch Davidian." http://www.bokus.com/bok/ 9781442208858/a-journey-to-Waco.com.

12. Ehow. "Rules of Engagement."ww.ehow.com/way_5659354_rules-engagement-military-use-force_. html#ixzz2Ol XmtTZD.

13. Emery, David. "Urban Legends. "Yellow Ribbon 'Tradition' Is of Recent Origin, Folklorists Say Symbol's history stretches back little more than 20 years." http//urbanlegends.about.com/cs/historical/a/yellowribbon.htm.

14. Fitzgerald, T-M. Emily's Robert E. Publish America, Maryland. May 2011.

15. G. Ed, Lcpl. MCRD. Yellow Footprints.Parris Island, 10April2009.http://www.recruitparents.com/boot camp/yellow.asp.

16. Laurain, Robin. Yahoo! Contributor Network. "How Did Tying Yellow Ribbons Become Popular in the United States? The Legacy of Tony Orlando and Dawn." www.yahoo.com.

17. Main Troop Greeters.www.mainetroopgreeters.com.

18. Montney. "Espirit de Corps". www.montney.com.marine/esprit.html.

19. News Herald Newspaper.http://www.news-herald.com/articles/2009/10/22/news/doc4adf07d03 d572 33 9296099.txtource.Unable to access original article.

20. Opentopia Online Encyclopedia. "What is the Croix de Guerre?" http://encycl. opentopia.com/term/Croix_ de _guerre.com

21. Operation Enduring Freedom—Operations.www.globalsecurity.org/military/ops/enduring-freedom-ops.htm.

22. Owens, Joseph. "Honoring the Beirut Peacekeepers: Never forget their sacrifice (Video)." October 23, 2012.www.examiner.com/article/honoring-the-beirut-peacekeepers-never-forget-their-sacrifice.

23. People Magazine, "Honoring the Fallen" December 28, 2009.pg. 154,.Time, Inc. Los Angeles, Ca.

24. Question Thread Deleted. http://answers.yahoo.com/question/index?qid=20081011114651AA CQnKy.

25. Talent, Eva. "What Are the Four Different Types of Military Operations?" http://www.ehow. com/info_ 8113615_four-different-types-military-operations.html#ixzz2PXEcv865.

26. Tomkins, Richard. "For Marines in Afghanistan; IED's are a Constant Fear." Published November 07, 2009 FoxNews.com http://www.foxnews.com/world/2009/11/07/marines-afghanistan-ieds-constant-fear/#ixzz2IM 4hwqVF.

27. Townsend, Mark." Point man in Afghanistan: a soldier's view." The Observer. Saturday, 31 March 2012. http://www.guardian.co.uk/world/2012/apr/01/point-man-soldier-Afghanistan.

28. Voices, "How Did Yellow Ribbons Become Popular?" http://voices.yahoo.com/how-did-tying-yellow-ribbons-become-popular-the-7516140.html?cat=75.

29. Webster, Merriam. "Webster's Online Dictionary." http://www.merriam-webster.com/dictionary.

30. Washington Post. "Article No Longer Accessible." http://www.washingtonpost.com/wp-dyn/content/article/2009/02/26/AR2009022602084.html.

END

Would you like to see your manuscript become a book?

If you are interested in becoming a PublishAmerica author, please submit your manuscript for possible publication to us at:

mybook@publishamerica.com

You may also mail in your manuscript to:

**PublishAmerica
PO Box 151
Frederick, MD 21705**

www.publishamerica.com

CPSIA information can be obtained at www.ICGtesting.com
Printed in the USA
LVOW13s2355170314

377781LV00001B/55/P